Pain, Pumpernickel & Profound Forgiveness

A Daughter's Story of Her Punishing & Loving Relationship with Her Father

Rosanne D'Ausilio, PhD

For more information, email drrosanne@gmail.com

ISBN: 979-8-9900160-0-2 - paperback
ISBN: 979-8-9900160-2-6 - ebook
ISBN: 979-8-9900160-1-9 - hardcover

I dedicate this book to my father up in Heaven who I'm certain is standing with his left hand on my right shoulder, a smile on his face and prideful tears rolling down his cheeks. I love you, Daddy.

Also By Rosanne

Foreword

I began drafting this book thirty years ago and for one reason or another, stopped. In the interim, I authored fifteen business books, which took up quite a bit of my time.

But I always wanted to write this book about my father. My original publisher (from my first book *Wake Up Your Call Center: Humanize Your Interaction Hub* which is now in its fourth edition), was very willing to publish the book. However, I was clear they (Purdue University Press) were not the proper publisher for this genre, so again, it went to the back burner.

As the years went by, the book fell off the stove—literally and figuratively. Through the many iterations of computers, I lost the file of the stories I had written. They were not on any floppy disk, CD drive, external hard drive, or any of my previous desktops.

So, I thought, 'OK, maybe the books I was destined to write were the business ones and not this one about my dad.' Or the process of writing was healing in and of itself.

In 2012, I put my house up for sale and moved from New York to Virginia, where my daughter resides. As I was clearing and cleaning out my office—a daunting task at best—between a bookcase shelf full of three-ring binders, I found a manila folder with a hard copy of the stories I had written about my father.

I stood there mesmerized, the hair on my arms sticking straight up, and at once was blessed with what was necessary for me to continue. Very slowly I began to input these vignettes. Usually, I could not do more than one per day as I got stimulated or triggered whenever I typed them. I was disciplined enough to only enter them into the computer, not edit, not embellish, but just get them into the computer, named, and into a folder called 'Dad Stories.'

Why did I write this book? Here are five reasons:

1. This book keeps the memories of my father alive for me and my family.

2. Hopefully, it'll strike a chord within you regarding your parents or family.

3. A wake-up call to the universe to not leave anything unsaid in your relationships.

4. A legacy to honor my family.

5. The possibility of acceptance, healing, forgiveness, and peace for me the writer, and you, the reader.

What follows is a collection of fifty plus vignettes of me and my father that help keep my memory of him alive and warms my heart. My hope is that my stories evoke memories for you of your parents or (fill in the blank) _____.

In this book, I share my experience, my journey to healing, which came about in spite of, or because of, me.

I include the best times, the worst times, the laughter, the tears, the wounds, the joys, the new perceptions, the healing, and the love. Allow me to take you on my journey and I hope you find yourself along the way and you get in touch with your own stories, don't hesitate to share them with me at rosanne@drrosanne.com

Contents

The final stage of healing is using what happens to you to help other people Gloria Steinem

- The Minds Journal

My Father the Tyrant

If I am writing about my dad, I thought I'd best give you background on who he was as a man, a husband, a breadwinner, a father, and my hero. What follows is the total of what I know about my father in terms of his childhood, history, or even likes and dislikes. He didn't like to talk about his childhood or anything about his life in Europe before coming to the United States.

Jack Alexander Miller was born in 1898 in Austria-Hungary. The lines of demarcation between the two countries were determined by whoever was in power at the time. He lived in a small town with his parents on a great deal of land. They farmed and had a general store and a bar on the premises. They had two teams of horses, one for everyday use and a special set for Sundays. My father attended boarding school in Budapest, staying with a family that provided him with room and board.

My father, who spoke little about his childhood in Europe, once told me, "People really respected my father. When he yelled out 'last call' in the bar, you could hear the chairs being moved back as if one chair only. They were in unison. They heard my father and so it was time to go. The metal of the bottom of the chairs on the wood floor resounded throughout the room."

He yearned to come to America. When he was sixteen his father finally relented and said yes. He was given $200—the equivalent of $7,000 today—and put on the last ship that sailed before World War I broke out. The SS *Vaterland* was the largest passenger ship in the world upon her completion. On the ship's maiden voyage, arriving at New York on May 21, 1914, there were 1,234 crew commanded by a commodore, four German Naval Reserve captains, and seven men as watch officers.

His father's house was taken over by the Nazis in the war. My dad said, "I don't ever want to go back. I want to remember it as it was. Anyhow, today the street doesn't even exist anymore." I visited the Czech Republic many years after his death. I felt like I was walking on the streets my father did, walking in his footsteps. It was a very special time for me. I went into the synagogue in Prague, the second-largest synagogue in Europe. As I walked down the center aisle and signed the guest book, I could almost feel my father's essence there.

He landed in NY, dressed in bell-bottom trousers and not speaking a word of English. He was met by a cousin and taken to Passaic, New Jersey, to live.

He was sent back to NY shortly thereafter to live with another set of cousins and to get a job, which he did. He would find workers for the factories and if hired, then he would get paid a dollar per worker. His favorite cousin, Sarah, taught him English and had quite a sense of humor. She told him to shake hands and say, "Go to Hell!" He did so until he learned differently.

He went to the 'school of hard knocks' sometimes holding two or three part-time jobs to make ends meet. But he was determined and tenacious. Each new job sat on the shoulders of the one that came before.

So, who was he? A man who felt blessed to be in America, responsible for himself and his family, and a man of his word. Whatever and whenever he spoke to you, you could take it to the bank. He was my first teacher of a set of principles with integrity as #1. He never used that word, not even sure he knew it, but he lived it. As you'll read in my Gall Bladder story, nothing got in the way of him keeping his word. I do not know many people who can say that and deliver it. My dad could and did. I am my word today from his role modeling.

He loved warm weather. My folks vacationed in Florida for ten years, sometimes being gone a month, only to return to working hard yet again. Once when he visited me in college in Coral Gables, we went to buy a typewriter (giving away my age) for me. While I was in the store comparing brands and prices, he was outside with his face pointed to the sun, holding onto a telephone pole so he wouldn't tip over, warming his bones. I inherited that trait from him too.

When children began to talk or talk back, my father had no use for them. He was very strict with me. There were lots of rules in our house. You couldn't talk at the dinner table—you were there to eat. You don't talk back to your mother or father. Children are to be seen and not heard. You don't get to have an opinion about anything, especially your mother's friends. It is the Golden Rule, the one that says, 'he who has the gold makes the rules.'

Introduction

BECAUSE SOME MEMORIES ARE simply inextricable from others, what follows are themes, topics, and threads. Writing this memoir for me was like seeing my father and myself through a different lens, one that has no boundaries, no rules, no barriers. It just is and flows and grows, soft like cotton and hard like steel.

Included are a few stories about my mother to present a total picture of my childhood, and to show that when I was scared or upset, I couldn't run to my mother for protection, safety, or support. It didn't exist.

The Photo

I SIT ON MY father's knee proud as a peacock. After all this is my daddy. I'm two years old and dressed in my custom-made yellow pinafore with white shoes and socks and a matching yellow ribbon in my long, curly, neatly combed brown hair. My father was sitting with a straight back and looking pridefully at our surroundings, loosely holding onto me so I would not fall off his lap. We were sitting on the top step leading up to our front door. It was a typical first house, colonial style, small lot, three small bedrooms on a street with similar houses. Early memories are not available in the present. Only a glimpse here and there.

"But how come he's not around much?" I question. "Where does he go all day long? Why isn't he here with me? I miss him. Is it my fault he's not here? Did I do something wrong? Was I a bad girl and so he went away? When he leaves, he tells me he'll see me later. What is later? When is that? Is it now? Is it this now? I'm just a little girl and I have so many questions."

I sit on my father's knee proud as a peacock. But I must sit just so or else, or else what? Something is missing here. Where is my smile? I am two years old but what is wrong with this picture? No spontaneity exists here. I am sitting very still and being a good little girl. Father probably said, "Act your age, young lady." What does that mean? How does a two-year-old act? "I'm not a big person, I'm a little girl!"

The truth is I have no memory of this photo being taken, nor who took it, yet there is no doubting its authenticity. With a deep sigh, I whisper to myself, "It would really be nice to know I sat on my dad's lap when I was little, even if it were just for a picture."

I strived to be the 'good girl,' but remember I was only two years old at the time. Something I was never allowed to be at two or twenty-two was human, to make mistakes. I felt when I made a mistake, which I did here and there, I was a mistake. When you have a critical mother and a rigid, scary father, you toe the line or else. And I didn't want to be subjected to the 'or else.'

Good Girl

ONE OF THE DEFINITIONS of 'good girl' is she stays within the guidelines and rules set for her. These fit me to a T. I learned fear early on. 'Be a good girl or else.' Harmless enough statement, or is it? Or else what? What would happen to me if I were 'bad?' Daddy or Mommy wouldn't love me or would punish me or leave me. So, I better be who they want me to be. If they wanted me to be green, I would be green. If they wanted me to be blue, I'd be blue. I learned this at an incredibly early age. It took me years to figure out who I was, a journey I still travel, as my self-image was determined by an outside force, my parents, for so many years.

I wanted to be a good girl, so I tried my best not to cry. However, when I got scared or hurt, what did I do? Yes, I cried. And then the famous, "Stop crying or I'll give you something to cry about" started. If (more likely when) I was being spanked, my father hit me harder.

Love was conditional: "If I were a good girl, then..."

Magazines

WHEN I WAS AT the height of my career, I was boasting about an article in a magazine about me. My father interrupted with, "But is there a man in your life?" I got mad, hurt, and lashed out, "You'd think you'd be proud of me that I can take care of myself and my children." He had no response that I can remember.

After my mother passed, I found a pile of magazines next to my mother's favorite chair in the living room by the sliding glass door overlooking the pool. The magazines were at least a foot high, and I was in each one of them, quoted in a story about the trade show I helped produce, pictures with the guest speaker, or my boss and me. Yet she never spoke of them, never acknowledged me in the stories, or mentioned having them let alone in a neat pile by her chair. In 1983 I had hired a local well-known, well-liked radio host as the guest speaker for one of the trade shows in Chicago. It was Oprah Winfrey. She was my luncheon speaker for two years in a row (for a fee of $3,000 each year). Then came *The Color Purple*, and the rest is history. No acknowledgment for this.

The Golden Rule(s)

ACCORDING TO MY FATHER, he who has the gold makes the rules, and that was him.

We were taught 'Don't talk about what goes on in the family outside our family.' I assumed all households were like mine. I found out many years later it was a wrong assumption.

My father was teaching me to stay within the lines in the coloring book story--don't make waves? Very loud lessons without speech. A boundaries lesson for a 'good girl.' My thoughts were 'If only they would tell me the rules. I would follow them to a T, but they're like shifting sand, they change without notice to me. Can't there be a Golden Rule Book? Is there no consistency in what's necessary? 'Tell me the rules and I'll follow them, and I'll go for the brass ring at the end.'

This is why as an adult I like chess so much. It's clear what moves, if any, each piece can and cannot move. Chess has rules and there are no mixed messages there.

But it didn't work that way in my family. I was 'damned if you do, damned if you don't' and it was a cycle that felt impossible to break. I learned early on to walk carefully on eggshells and do my best to be unseen.

"Finish what's on your plate. People in Europe are starving." I didn't question him and thus became a member of the Clean Plate Club of which I have, it seems, a lifetime membership.

My father had a ferocious temper and it worked. It kept me in line. I was afraid of him for most of my early years. There was only one side of a story for him, and it was his. If there were somehow two sides, they were both his.

One morning as I came downstairs for elementary school, my coloring book was on the dining room table, opened to a page with a picture of large animals on it outlined in one color, deep red, and then shaded inside the lines with a lighter shade of red. My father did that! I was shocked. He also started jigsaw puzzles and did the outline, the edges and then filled in the center. Suddenly, my father became human to me. Yet when we did these two things together, there was never a conversation. I see now the lesson was planted to not make waves. Contain your thoughts, Rosanne, and be a 'good girl.'

When Kevin was born, my father would arrive unannounced at our apartment early every morning with a bag of bagels. He said, "Good morning" sheepishly, "I brought breakfast." He was very vulnerable as they were his ruse to gain entrance to see this newborn baby, Kevin. It was very sweet, and the bagels were very fresh. He was a grandfather and there were different rules for them it seemed. My father got Kevin's name mixed up. He called him Rosanne here and there, remembering when I was born. The bottom line is he was loving the birth and their special times together.

Fast forward to a visit when Kevin was ten and Kim, my daughter, age six, and we were eating dinner.

My father said, "We don't talk at the dinner table. We're here to eat. Eat what's on your plate." I took a deep breath and said, "Well at our dinner table we do talk. And we eat our meal as well. It's our time to be together as a family and talk about our day."

He mumbled, "Well, eat your dinner."

When my children, Kevin and Kim, and I get back home from visiting my parents we sit down for dinner. I say to them as I was taught, "Eat, people in Europe are starving." Kevin says, "Mom, how is it that they do not starve if I eat all that's on my plate?" Truth telling here, I didn't know what to say. I don't have any answer, so I just said, "Eat your dinner." To this day I don't know the answer and always wondered what people do who live in Europe. What do they tell their children to get them to finish what's on their plates? I asked a friend of mine who grew up in Germany and she said, "Eat what is on your plate, some people have no food."

Children are to be seen and not heard. I'm a young girl, maybe eight or so, and I am along on a visit to my parents' friends. I had to sit quietly, not fidget, and most importantly, if I'm offered anything I am to say no. And I did as ordered.

When the woman, Edith, offered me cookies and milk, I said, "No, thank you." Edith said, looking at my mother, "It's OK to let the kid have something." I repeated, "No, thank you" or there'd be hell to pay later. Of course, I wanted the cookies. They smelled of the chocolate in the chocolate chips maybe still warm from the oven.

I googled 'How were children raised in the 1940s?' I was surprised to see in writing: 'The 1940s and 1950s were characterized more by authoritarian parenting. Men ruled the roost at work and women commanded the household with an iron fist. Mothers were admonished not to spoil their children, who were expected to be seen and not heard.' My family exactly, and I had been taking it personally!

Brownie

WHEN I WAS BORN, Brownie, part collie, part German shepherd, was already in our family. My mom got him as a pup, and he was a few years old when I came into the picture. I loved him so much. He was my babysitter. My mom would go into the grocery store, leaving the baby carriage outside with me in it and Brownie guarding. When my baby carriage was sold, the new owner called and said, "Excuse me, but do you have a dog? He seems to have followed us all the way home." They lived several miles away. That was Brownie. He thought I was in the carriage and that they were taking me away.

He was my companion. I tied him to my tricycle in the warm weather and we played in the snow in the winter. When I would get scared of a sound or an unidentified noise, Brownie was allowed to sleep in my room. Otherwise, his domain was the basement.

We had Brownie until he was fourteen. I remember it like it was yesterday. I was playing ball in the street and there was barking a few doors down. There was a bulldog that attacked Brownie. Brownie was bleeding from the mouth. I ran home to my mother, "Quick, come, something is wrong with Brownie."

We took Brownie to the animal hospital, but he never came out. He had a heart attack. Well, I wouldn't come out either, not for two weeks. I was so upset that I couldn't tell the complete story without crying.

As any normal child, I kept bringing home puppies, and kittens, and, with begging eyes asked "Mommy, please, please can we keep this dog/cat?" She said, "No, you don't take care of them. And I don't want to care for another animal." "But I didn't get a chance." I said, "Brownie was here before me!" Back I went to return the puppy or kitten to wherever I got it. I was damned if I do and damned if I don't from a very young age.

Cheese Delkas aka Cheese Danish

My mother was making cheese delkas what we would loosely call cheese Danish today except the outside of ours was flaky and the insides tasted much better. I googled but couldn't find the word 'delka', but my father was from Austria-Hungary, and I suspect it came from there, though I have no information to support it.

I had a very important job. I was five years old, and I was the official Taster. We worked in silence, my mom and I; I at the ready when it was time to taste.

I loved the cheese ones. She also made prune ones using lekvar which is Hungarian for prune butter—but the cheese was the best. To this day I don't know what farmer's cheese is. Google says, 'Farmer cheese is a pressed cottage cheese that is slightly more acidic and has a firmer texture, thanks to a lower moisture content.' It sounds terrible and yet it was sweet and delicious, not like this definition sounds. I'm sure Mom used eggs and sugar to make it just so. That was my favorite taste except for the finished product.

While mom was working the dough I wasn't needed. I sat in front of a cabinet nearby and opened it slowly. Then I took out the pots and pans and lids and played cooking along with mom. When she was ready for me, I stopped what I was doing and ran to taste it. Yummy, so good.

After they baked and were put aside to cool, I had the job of shaking the powdered sugar—not too much—across the tops. I only got to taste and eat just one delka, but it was worth the wait.

The smell of cooked cheese, the flaky dough, having been witness to the production, and my importance as the Taster, all added to the experience of that first bite. Most importantly, my mom and I were doing something together on a quiet sunny Saturday morning. Few words were spoken, which only added to the intimacy of the experience, and it remains a very special memory of my mom for me.

Weekends

IMAGINE BEING ASLEEP AND in that almost-awake state you sense someone is there, someone is watching you. And there was and he was. My father stood at my door and watched me sleep until I felt it and he said, "Are you going to sleep all day? You are so lazy. Get up now." I was so afraid of his rage that I did as he said. But why? I didn't have to go or be anywhere, it was the weekend.

All the days were the same for my father. He wore his white-on-white short-sleeved dress shirt with his initials on the pocket, JAM, and his leisure clothes were khaki pants. He would turn over in his grave before he'd put on a pair of jeans, especially ones with holes or tears or if they were miscolored. Nor would he pay the exorbitant price for these 'disasters.'

Every Sunday at 5 pm. my parents called to see how we were. "How are the kids? How is work? What's the weather like? Anything new?" The call rarely lasted more than five minutes. They were like recorded announcements and my father was paying. Long-distance charges applied.

Visiting Days & Brunch at Home

WHEN I WAS YOUNG, somewhere between three and six years old, our family got dressed up and went to visit my parents' friends on Sundays. Sometimes we went to homes where I had to sit quietly and not fidget. If I were offered something, I was to say, "No, thank you."

My fondest memories are of going to visit my Aunt Betty and Uncle George. Of course, they weren't really relatives, but it was respectful and polite to call them aunt and uncle. They lived in a big farmhouse with a porch that wrapped around the entire outside. The house was situated on land adjacent to a large working farm. It took about an hour to get there. In those days, it was considered quite a trip. We packed hard-boiled eggs, buttered rye bread, and red, ripe, beefsteak tomatoes and halfway there, we pulled off the road, had our lunch, and then proceeded on our trip.

Once we arrived, I said hello and was off. I went to the farm and played with the cows, the horses, the Lassie dog who wrapped his paws around my leg as I climbed stairs, and any animal that would stay still long enough for me to pet it. I don't have a memory of any people around, but the peace and joy I felt with the animals have remained with me to this day.

Sunday brunches were a tradition in our house, and an incredibly special time because it was just my father and me going to his cousin's bakery. Because we were relatives, we were allowed in the back where all the wonderful smells and sounds were. Here is where we chose a hot-out-of-the-oven pumpernickel bread. It was too hot to slice and was the size of an exceptionally large watermelon. Normally it was cut, carved in half, horizontal to the ground, and then in half again. Ultimately one of those last pieces is what we took home.

Adding to this delicious memory was the expert way in which the breads were handled by craftsmen, not just bakers of breads. Reverently and with pride and expertise, they were offered as gifts of love, manna from Heaven. I was maybe ten years old and remember it all so vividly as if it were just yesterday.

What also grabbed my attention was the precise preparation of coconut bars. I thought everyone knew what they were, but it was not true. Only Ohio residents or visitors, and maybe only those in or from Cleveland where I was born knew what they were.

What is a coconut bar? For those of you not from Cleveland, imagine, if you will, a white or yellow cake cut into the size of a quarter-pound stick of butter, dipped ever so carefully in warm, melted chocolate, and then rolled in coconut. A work of art. Then the final task was to place them gently on parchment paper two inches apart and ready for sale. I don't know which is better, the process or the eating of it, both mesmerized me. I have never seen them anywhere else but from this one bakery.

Now Dad and I are in the car heading home and I'm holding the bag with this wonderful, warm, sweet-smelling half football bread in my lap, patiently or not so patiently, (remember I'm ten), wanting to get home quickly and dig in.

It was the same every Sunday, hand-sliced, warm pumpernickel bread cut only by my father with the same precision as he would give to a Thanksgiving turkey, creamed herring with extra sour cream and onions added, and cottage cheese and lots of butter for the bread. My father taught me a very serious lesson. With fresh, warm, just-baked bread, you need lots of butter, and then you watch it disappear as it melts into the bread.

My mother never came with us; she stayed home and prepared for our return. This was a sacred, special time for me to be with my dad. No big discussions, no words were even exchanged, it was just our time to be together.

One weekend when I was about eleven, my mother was out somewhere, and it was just me and my father home. I was hungry and wanted to make SpaghettiOs.

Here's what happened. "Dad, I want to eat something. Can I make SpaghettiOs?" He replied, "No, wait until your mother gets home." "No," I whined, "I'm hungry now. I know how to make it, you know. Please?" He relented and I opened and emptied the can, filled it with water, emptied it into the pot and put it on the stove. "Oh no," I said just above a whisper. "Is there a problem?" my father asked. "Um, I forgot you don't put water in the can." "Well sit down and eat it since you know how to cook it!" my father said and stood there while I tried to swallow a spoonful.

My father worked six days a week and when he came home at 6:30 or 7:00 for dinner, there was always a hot meal awaiting my father every night, even on weekends. Always fresh, never leftovers, including fresh bread, never store-bought wrapped in plastic. We had fresh rye bread with caraway seeds, pumpernickel on Sundays, and challah (a white braided loaf, what we called holiday bread). There was no Chinese, Italian, or Thai food, nor any stews or casseroles in our house. Meals consisted of meat, baked or mashed potatoes, and a veggie.

When he was traveling and, on the road, my mother and I would order Chinese food or eat popcorn or corn on the cob for dinner, having the flexibility that did not exist when he was home.

My mother nightly prepared the coffee, followed by my father making it and his own breakfast in the morning. When my mother woke, she only had to reheat the coffee. She didn't eat breakfast, just drank black coffee daily.

My Sister

I HAD A SISTER sixteen years older than me, Elaine. I called her Sissie because when I was little, I tried for 'sister' and Sissie stuck. We were very close, but she got married when I was four, so it was as if I were an only child.

My mother was forty years old and her only child, my sister, was about to graduate high school and there was my mother's freedom in reach. Then she got pregnant by mistake. She wanted a boy—Ronald would be his name. My sister said, "What if it's a girl?" Mom said, "No, it's going to be a boy" and here I am. I'm told I was a very good baby, that I slept through the night the first week. I have no early memories, a picture here or there of me sitting very still with a half-smile on my face as if the photographer was trying to get me to smile.

I was the second born so money was more available when a second child came along. We lived in a house, not an apartment. We had two cars in the family as compared to my sister who was raised in an apartment and there was one car in the family.

During my divorce, we were having dinner at my sister's house. Her three grown children, ten years or so younger than me, and their children close in age to mine were all present. I raised my wine glass to toast my family and express my gratitude for their loving support and started with: "Thank you so much for your support and love during this horrendous time for me." To my chagrin, tears welled up in my eyes. My vision blurred; the food I had just chewed and swallowed seemed to be stuck in my throat. My hands and face began to perspire. I tried my best to hold back the tears. Too late.

The room went silent; it felt like no one was exhaling. It was as if no one had ever seen an adult cry before. My sister was quickly making excuses for me to her children and grandchildren as if I were not present. My children, used to me crying, had no problem with it. Had my sister not made an issue of it, I don't believe any of the kids would have minded in the least. Once again, I was 'too emotional.'

One Thanksgiving we were going to my sister's home for turkey dinner. We piled into the car—yes, that same Cadillac—me, my dad, and Kim and Kevin. Going to her house for any meal was an adventure. Now here is a fact, not a rumor or even a bad joke. My sister wasn't a very good cook. We said we'd stop on the way to eat because either the food wouldn't be good, or the turkey would never get cooked (this happened twice). It became our private joke: 'Where should we go to eat on the way to dinner at my sister's?' The belly laughs lasted a good five minutes.

I, on the other hand, cooked like my mother, who was a good cook. My father's favorite from me was a grilled cheese sandwich with French fries. The grilled cheese was with American cheese and rye bread fried in butter, browned, flipped, and more butter, browned, and eaten. Couldn't be bad with all that butter, but he loved it, and I loved making it for him. He liked me to cut it into quarters, almost bite size—he thought they lasted longer.

When he was in his last week, I had the privilege to be with him. He was ninety-four and in his freezer were separately wrapped packages of a leg of roasted chicken, a container filled with homemade mashed potatoes (with that butter again), and peas or corn in small Tupperware containers. He told me, "I save these all for my Sunday meals and I take out one portion of chicken, one potato, and one serving of peas, and I have a wonderful Sunday supper all thanks to you." When he passed, one of the hardest things was opening the freezer and having to toss those individual portions of the packaged food I had prepared.

The Stepford Family

WE WERE WHAT I believed was a traditional family with the roles clear that my father was our provider, and my mother took care of the house. She did take the laundry to a Hungarian woman as my father was very fussy about his shirts. He wanted them ironed, put on a hanger, and no starch.

From the outside looking in, we did look like the perfect family, a nice colonial house in a good neighborhood, the yard manicured and taken care of.

We were the Stepford family. We did look the part, but I felt empty inside. My mother would come home from wherever she was, perhaps playing golf, spending time with a friend, getting fresh bread for dinner, and just in time to prepare the evening meal.

At about ten years old I took piano lessons. My hands were too small to reach an octave, so my teacher adjusted for this. I participated in recitals, and I have a faint memory of my parents being there. I have no recollection of receiving a "Good girl."

I didn't like the lessons, but my parents did. They thought it looked good on their resume of the 'perfect family.' I didn't like my teacher or the two buses I had to take to get to his house and then two to get back home.

I was an overachiever in school and in my work life. I got kudos from teachers and bosses, but I was missing ones from my parents.

To the outside world they spoke highly of me, but behind closed doors pointed out all I did wrong. They found fault with me so often and consistently that I believed them. With no outlet to share any of these stories with, I believed what they told me. After all, these were my parents and they loved me.

I was married to my children's father for fourteen years and had Kevin and Kim. Except for these wonderful children, the marriage was a mistake from the start.

When I told my parents my husband and I were getting divorced, my mother requested, "Please don't say anything to the people in our apartment building." She was shaming me for getting divorced even though she wasn't fond of the man. There was no support for getting out of an abusive relationship. Here my father joined in as they both had an investment in looking good.

I was divorced with two young children when I met and married Tony ten years later. We had a fifty-person wedding gala at a restaurant set up like a greenhouse on Long Island, New York. We had the carpet draped in white so that my father could walk me down the aisle, which he did. There was not a dry eye in the room, including me. And I wore white. My mother had said (hoping for a "No, of course not"), "You're not going to wear white, are you?"

To which I responded, "Yes, Mom, I am. This person standing before you has never been married before!" She was quiet and had no response. I was single for ten years before this day and did a lot of work on myself so I wouldn't make the same mistakes—others, maybe—but not the same ones.

As the evening progressed, dancing began, and for the first time ever—not even at my first wedding—I danced with my father. For me, this was a very touching moment. It was as if we danced together for the (first and) last time as he handed me over to dance with my new husband.

From what my mother had told me, my father wasn't a dancer. They never went dancing and had few weddings to attend so the occasions didn't present themselves. So how special was he to dance with me at my wedding? After all, this wasn't one of those formal ones with a big band that announced, "Please welcome Mr. and Mrs. So-and-So," then invited the bride and groom to dance, afterward the father of the bride and the bride. No, that wasn't the kind of wedding we had.

But the specialness of it for me was the intimacy, all the loving support of friends and family present to witness our love, and then that cheek-to-cheek dance (so the photographer could get both our faces) lives on in my memory of that day.

In retrospect, I can see how invested in the outcome my mother was on both occasions. If we had a conversation today, I think we could laugh about it, although I did carry the lingering pain of being 'not ok' and 'different.'

Those were her issues and of the moment. Not mine. The tool of 'How important will this be in one year, in six months, in three months, in one month, today?' comes to mind. It was not important in the scheme of things. It was the perfect time to let it go. What a freeing concept and experience.

Stop crying or...

"Stop crying or I'll give you something to cry about!" "Nobody likes a crybaby!" "Don't cry over spilled milk." "You're too emotional." "You wear your heart on your sleeve." From an early age, it was clear these weren't admirable attributes, but rather serious judgments and criticisms. In other words, 'no no's.' But where is the line for determining what is 'too emotional? I don't know but I seem to have passed it.

These were standard accusations to my tears when I was a child. It was very clear that crying was not permitted, tolerated, or OK on any level. Beyond that, emotions very clearly were a sign of weakness. They were to be kept under tight control.

In any relationships I had, male or female, if I got 'too emotional' they would say "Get a grip on yourself. Why are you crying? What's wrong now? "Nobody likes a crybaby. What's wrong with you?"

When I was very young my mother's brother died. I came home from elementary school and found her sitting in the green overstuffed easy chair in the living room all curled up crying. When I asked what was wrong, she told me Uncle Jack had died. I didn't know him, but it was still very sad. When my father came home and found my mother still in the same chair, still crying, he told her there was nothing she could do about it. "Don't cry over spilled milk!" Ah, so the rules weren't just about children crying, adults were treated the same way.

I was the first in my family to go to college. My sister went to business school. As I was inching forward to board the plane, my dad was hugging and kissing me with tears rolling down his face as if a faucet were opened full force. He was repeating over and over, "I love you so much, I am going to miss you. I love you." My first thought was, 'Who is this man and what did you do with my father?' In a short time, I was repeating the words back to him.

What stopped this interaction was the line—we had reached the front of the boarding door for the Cleveland to Miami yo-yo flight that went up and down and made about six stops along the way. I distinctly remember my pageboy hair falling stop by stop as the humidity increased. By the time we reached Florida, my hair was straight, and my eyes were puffy from all my tears. As I recall, everyone else on the plane kept their distance. Not one person asked me if I was OK. After all, 'nobody likes a crybaby.'

As an adult when I cried, I was unable to speak and cry at the same time. My innermost thought was once I start, I'll never stop. What stopped me and had such a grip on my not crying or not talking about it was it was against the rule 'don't talk about what goes on in our family outside our family.'

Then I went through stages of crying. I could mouth words, but no sound came out. Next, I could speak and cry, but you couldn't differentiate what I was saying from the wailing. I then graduated to being able to speak and cry softly, and today I can speak and not cry, even if the tears are overflowing. This was and is a breakthrough for me.

However, whenever I said goodbye to my parents after a Florida visit, there were tears aplenty. It was as if we all saved our tears for the very last minute, not in the house before we left, not on the ride to the airport, but as I was getting the luggage out of the trunk of the car curbside at the airline. It was Waterfall City then.

Somehow, these were OK tears. I never was able to figure out what the difference was. I could only cry in my parents' arms and listen to what they said. Both said, "Thank you so much for coming. Call when you get home. We love you and will miss you so much. Don't forget to call us Sunday at 5 p.m." No words would form, let alone come out of my mouth. My heart was swollen with love and fear, fear that I would never see them alive again. And I'd bet they had the same thoughts ruminating in their heads. Because of my progress with tears, I was able to hug them with tears running down my face and tell them how much I loved them too.

Making wedding arrangements with my first husband's family was very emotional for me. I cried during the entire meeting. My soon-to-be-husband said, "Don't pay any attention to her. She just does this. She's fine. Really. Just give her a minute." However, they looked at me as if I had tentacles and were from another planet.

The catharsis of getting the tears out felt wonderful to me. On the other hand, the intensity of them still throws me sometimes to this day. The depth of my sadness, the source of which is unknown to me now, scares me. I sometimes feel like a tire whose air is being let out a little at a time. Better than to keep it in. I see I have work to do in this area. I do believe it's an ongoing process.

Silence is Golden, or Is It?

HAVE YOU EVER HAD the experience of being with someone and feeling that space is sacred, safe, and special, that no words were needed? I have too, albeit those times are rare but memorable. It felt like if you spoke, it would take away from the moment.

The opposite is an uncomfortable silence, felt as stress, anger, and sometimes fear. At the very least, it's like walking on eggshells and not knowing what to do or say. Taken to an extreme, you might think it was your fault. I experienced all of these in this book, in these vignettes, and especially in this story.

I reread my bakery story where my father and I were on our Sunday excursion. 'But where are the conversations, the words, even any mindless chatter?' I asked myself. I couldn't recall any. These father and daughter events were so special to me and yet, there were no words.

This is a common occurrence in my memories of the time spent with my father.

We were on our way to the synagogue on the second day of Rosh Hashanah. It was a mild Fall Day with the leaves just starting to flutter from the trees and crunch under our feet as we walked from the parking lot. I had the honor and privilege every year from when I was about twelve of going with my father only. My mother was home cooking for us, having gone with him the night before.

I say 'honor and privilege' because children weren't allowed in the main sanctuary. There were classrooms with folding chairs set up for the children.

The main room had soft velvet chairs with armrests in a deep, dark, cranberry color, and were all attached like in a movie theatre. When I was in that chapel, I felt like I was in a holy, sacred space. Everywhere you looked there were elder Jewish men and women quietly speaking to one another before the service began. I only had entry because I was with my father. I witnessed him saying the prayers and following along in the prayer book. I never knew my father could read Hebrew and yet, there he was amongst the best of them. It sounded like mumbling interfaced with song, even chanting at times. He had his talis (prayer shawl) around his neck, a beautiful white silk embroidered shawl with tassels. This talis came out for the Jewish holidays. Otherwise, it was stored in a zipper-locked, square-shaped blue-velvet-on-the-outside, silk-feeling-on-the-inside bag.

I loved going with my father and sharing this wonderful spiritual experience. I felt such peace and connection with something larger than life. It felt like I should whisper if I were to speak. There was a serenity I had never experienced before. But again, I have no memory of talking, of any conversation between us. When he chatted with people he knew—my parents were founding fathers, called charter members, of this temple—he introduced me but that was it. When it was just the two of us, the silence was very loud.

On a few occasions as an adult, I went to the racetrack with my father. Again, my mother stayed home. I was all dressed up this one time in a white suit, purple silk long-sleeved blouse with the collar of the blouse folded over the collar of the jacket, purple high heels and we were 'off to the races.' I loved the smell of horses, always having wanted a pony when I was little. Most of the people were dressed up and I could feel the nervous or excited tension all around.

It was intense as people waited and watched and yelled and screamed or cursed if they lost. The only conversation with my dad was, "Did you win?" He said, "No, did you?" or "Yes, did you?" In the car on the way home, silence again.

As adults, any conversations were about work mostly. I remember sitting on a sunbed at his pool in Florida and telling him about this great idea I had. I was very animated as I sat up almost out of the sunbed. He interrupted with, "And how much money does that put in your pocket?" To me, this translated as 'it's a stupid idea.' I felt like he put a pin in me like a balloon. I laid back down on the sunbed, deflated, and with hurt feelings.

The sad news is he never changed. He was so wrapped up in money and responsibility, he was not able to receive and process another way of being.

Looking back now that he's passed, it's clear to me that my father didn't know how to speak to children. Not all children. Up to two years old he's great with kids, but once they could talk, and especially talk back, he didn't know what to say. But I think it was more that he had no role models for talking to kids other than, of course, "How is school" and rote conversations like that which are over in two seconds.

He also didn't know how to talk to adult children other than to criticize or impose his belief systems.

At one time we lived in a very large house in Danbury, CT. When my mother saw it for the first time, she said, "How long before you sh** this place up?" Whenever she could, she got a dig in sometimes over or under a compliment. It is what Fritz Perls would say are cold fuzzies, a criticism sitting on a compliment. It was a beautiful house, with five bedrooms, three baths, and an above-ground pool. This was where we lived for fourteen years before downsizing and moving back to New York.

To Beat or Not to Beat

"QUICK EVERYONE, YOU MUST come and hear this." We were about twenty or so men and women divided into groups of four to five. Everyone came scrambling into the main room to the group therapy session I was participating in.

As everyone was seated and focused, Fritz said, "Please tell your story again, Rosanne." And so, I did.

"When I was a child and I did something unacceptable according to my mother, I had to stand in the corner of the kitchen facing the wall and I wasn't allowed to speak. This was how she disciplined me. It wasn't until my father came home from work that I was 'rescued,' told to apologize to my mother, and life went on. He was my Get Out of Jail Free Card."

I did this routine and that was the end of it. However, when she couldn't 'control me,' she tattled on me to my father. She actually set me up for what follows. Now he had to take serious action. She knew this and was a silent accomplice.

In a special place in the upstairs hallway between the two bedrooms, I got whacked with his belt with him saying, "This hurts me more than it hurts you." 'How is that so?' I asked myself. 'I'm the one getting struck.' His typical, count-on-able response was "Stop crying, or I'll give you something to cry about!" My father was famous for his one-liners. "If it were not for me, you wouldn't be here." I could scream at my mother with liberal consequences, not so with my father. Out would come the belt and like 'a bad girl,' I would follow him upstairs, head hanging low, knowing what was coming next.

What's of primary importance here is as I was explaining my childhood to the others in the group, I said, "It wasn't such a big deal; it was only when I was really bad." That was the point when Fritz called us all together to hear my 'contaminated mind,' my 'contaminated thinking.' I had been brainwashed to believe it was OK to beat a child if they were 'bad.' My bad, by the way, was talking back to my mother. I was a good girl, albeit walking on eggshells to keep it that way, and sometimes my behavior was incorrect. There was never a distinction between my behavior and me. It wasn't 'my behavior is unacceptable.' It landed on me that I was unacceptable. I felt like there was something inherently wrong with me.

This was when the light bulb went off, my ah-ha moment, as I realized no child deserves to be beaten no matter what. It took me to adulthood to have this seep into my brain and then believe it. To this I can now add, "I make mistakes, but I am not a mistake." This is my powerful one-liner!

By way of background, I participated in a Gestalt therapy workshop created by one of the founders, Fritz Perls (1893-1970). What is Gestalt therapy? It is a form of psychotherapy centered on increasing a person's awareness, freedom, and self-direction. It focuses on the present moment rather than past experiences and often uses role-playing to aid the resolution of past conflicts.

What I remember most about Fritz was he lived in this wonderful round house about an hour north of New York City. We had the workshop in this house. There were no chairs; just large pillows in the outer circle of the room, enough for each of us to sit on. And he, Fritz, was a very powerful, grounded, very loving, supportive human being and an awesome therapist.

My first reaction to being made the center of attention was the feeling there was something wrong with me. That led to a release of shame and blame, and a new construct around child discipline. No coincidence that I was brought up to be perfect and if I weren't, well, the other end of the pendulum isn't a pretty sight. I lived unconsciously between the two. It was a setup from the start in that we are human which inherently implies we will make mistakes. However, we are not, I am not, a mistake!

Hung for a Lion When I was a Lamb

I HAD FOUR INCIDENTS at three different times in my life that stand out for when I was wrongly blamed. You tell me what you think.

It's pre-kindergarten and we are at recess. Suddenly, I burst out crying. "Help me, please," I cry to the teacher. "Do something. It hurts. Look at my foot." I'd gotten stung by a bee, and it was swelling up and hurt really bad.

The school, of course, immediately called my mother to come and get me and take me to the ER or the doctor. Well, my mother was busy and so by the time she got to me, I felt like I'd pass out and die.

She didn't speak to me on the way home. The silence was so loud; she was so mad. I interrupted whatever it was she was doing and somehow it was my fault.

It was Easter time. I was in kindergarten or first grade. We were coloring eggs to take to school. Mom had given me some to take in the morning. When I came home for lunch I took some more eggs, ones I independently helped myself to from the refrigerator. After school I put the shoes with my colored eggs on the stairs to be taken up to my room later.

With no clue as to why it was happening, the eggs began to run out of the shoes and ever so slowly slide down the carpeted steps, one slimy step at a slimy time. No one ever told me that the eggs had to be hard boiled. I was only a child, what did I know! Boy was mom mad.

Fast forward a couple of years and the people across the street got a sweet little puppy. I went to pet the dog and he jumped up and bit me just under my eye. I came running home to my mother. "Mommy, help, I just got bitten by that dog. Help, I can barely see."

Mom took me to the doctor who said, "Do you know how lucky you are, young lady? Another inch and you could have lost your eye!"

Mother was having a dinner party that night and she did not have time for this and, of course, it was my fault because I touched the dog.

Fast forward again to when I was sixteen. I was on a double date, and we were on our way to the movies. My date and I were sitting in the back seat. I was behind the driver when a car sped right through an intersection, never stopped at the stop sign, and smashed into the car right where I was sitting. I passed out and when I came to, the police were helping me out of the car. "Come, young lady, we'll get you tended to, it's going to be OK. You're going to be OK." I was taken to the hospital, and while waiting on a gurney, we all called our parents. I had a strict curfew and wasn't going to get home in time, so I needed to report in. My left leg, specifically my knee, had gotten stuck underneath the driver's seat.

The other girl's parents came to get us and took me home. They helped me walk into the house as my leg was so sore. My parents thanked them, so appreciative of helping me. When they left, I got screamed at. "What's wrong with you? This is all your fault. Why did you have to go out with that boy? You're grounded!"

Neither of them asked how I felt or how badly my leg hurt. Where was the compassion, worry, and caring that I was OK? Nonexistent.

My listening, reinforced by their consistency, said it was my fault. I can't do anything right. Again, I'm a disappointment.

These isolated incidents carry the angst of 'there is something innately very wrong with me. I can't do anything right.' From an early age—preschool—it was embedded in me consciously and unconsciously. I was hung for a lion when I was a lamb.

Mommy Dearest

As a teenager when I wanted to wear what all the girls were wearing, my mother said, "You can't wear what they wear, you have to wear what looks good on you." This was aimed at my being overweight, always being put on diets, and treated as if she—I can't say 'they'—were ashamed of me. And of course, not wanting to feel that shame, I stuffed the feelings with food. For many years I had an eating issue. I would stuff my feelings, good or bad, with food.

My parents used to go to Florida on vacation once a year for several weeks when I was in my teens. On their return there were presents, of course, but never, never clothes. When I asked my mother why, she said, "I can't bring you clothes because I don't know what size you'll be when we're back." I can still hear her voice in my head saying this each time I put on weight.

I finally have my weight under control and am petite, but I do think I have dysmorphia and am just waiting for it to ramp up. And it has ramped up over the years, going up and down. I'm pleased to report that for the last ten years or so it's within five pounds, not the forty or fifty I was famous for. It's taken what it's taken for me to look in the mirror and see me, not my defects.

For my seventy-fifth birthday, we planned a big party in the Dominican Republic and an opportunity to dress up. I found a beautiful brown cocktail dress and I decided to buy it even though the event was a year away. I heard my mother's voice so loud she could have been standing next to me. "How can you buy a dress a year ahead when you'll just gain weight, and it won't fit." I took a deep breath and bought the dress. The following year on my birthday I wore the dress, and it still fits to this day. The fact that it was brown was also something special. My mother said I was too dark to wear brown. It's one of my favorite colors today.

"Stay out of the sun. You are getting too dark. It doesn't look nice, you know. Your elbows, your knuckles, and your knees look especially dirty! Good girls don't get that dark!" This was my mother barking at me.

Mother and I were in Hallandale, Florida, just south of Fort Lauderdale preparing for my first wedding at age twenty-five (going on fourteen emotionally). I tan easily and loved the sun as a child. It warmed my bones and when I really baked in it, I felt at one with the sun. It felt as if the sun were breathing me, not the other way around. However, my reverie was interrupted with. "What color polish do you think would look good with those fingers, especially those dark knuckles?" My mother asked the nail lady. Again, the hands were too dark. "They didn't look as if they had ever been washed." She was like a broken record.

I was sent to the beauty parlor for color testing for manicures. No reds— they really made those knuckles dirty-looking, and after a day, the polish turned purple because there was so much blue in the reds. Mauve and beige didn't even show up. Finally, a soft pink was acceptable to Mommie Dearest.

These were constant recorded announcements from mother. She had it in her mind that my coloring was too dark. And to take it to the limit that this was somehow a reflection on her. On me, according to her, a tan didn't look like a tan, it looked dirty. Never mind that people complimented me and were often envious of the soft brown the sun's rays gave me.

For most of my early years, I was as brown as a bunny. As a child, I was lovingly teased and called Little Beaver. When vacation time came, and Florida was the destination, the beach and the sun and the fresh air were sought after. There is no smell like that of the ocean, the fresh saltwater, the sound of the water as it slaps the shore and the tide coming in and out. Toes in the sand, the sun baking on my body. Elbows, knuckles, and knees held no importance in those days.

But as an adult, the roles seemed to change.

Primping in the mirror, I had an ongoing conversation with myself. 'I can't do anything right, let alone get a tan. I really like the way I tan the first day out. I feel toasty warm by the sun and the world is my oyster. My cheeks and nose get rosy. My face gets tight, and wrinkles disappear. I look healthy and feel more alive. My large brown eyes shine brightly. I use little makeup and my hair looks even better. My jean shorts and white tank top nicely show off my new color.'

One would think that mother had pearly white skin since she had such a position about tan. Not so. She was dark-complexioned but when she tanned, hers was the right color. Her tan was this reddish, golden, almost Native American color that was truly beautiful. No dark knuckles, knees, or elbows for mother.

Father, on the other hand, rarely said anything judgmental to or about me. Not about my tan, my weight, nothing that genuinely mattered to me. He was very accepting of who I was and how I looked and always found something to compliment. For the minutia that happens daily, he left that to my mother. In retrospect, his silence spoke volumes!

Father loved the sun as much as I did and would sit for hours basking in it, never using any suntan lotion or oil. For us in those days, the sun was healing; the reflection on our bodies warmed our bones. It calmed us and quieted the thoughts running around in our minds like the ticker tape at Times Square. It was meditative and peaceful.

As the day of my wedding approached, my mother was constantly vigilant to make sure that the degree of color was not too much. To be clear here, not the nail polish, me. The audience at the wedding would surely notice if I were too dark and then hold it against mother. What kind of mother would let her daughter get so dark? Where are her values? She is much too lax. What is wrong with her? Tsk tsk tsk. The newspaper will print, "She was a beautiful bride, but she stayed in the sun too long. Even the picture reflects dark knuckles and knees. How could her mother let her do that to herself, especially on her wedding day? Too bad."

My father was silent through all this as he called it 'women's work.'

Never mind the people who said I was a beautiful bride, what did they know anyway!

Brother, Can You Spare a Dime

MY FATHER FOUND ERNST Mueller in the telephone book. He dialed the number carefully, took a deep breath, waited, and questioned the person who answered, "Hello, are you by any chance Ernst Mueller?"

The man hesitantly and skeptically said, "Yes, I am."

My father continued, "Are you the Ernst Mueller that has a brother in the United States?"

Once more, he answered reticently but now also curiously, "Yes, I am."

With unbridled excitement in his voice, my father said, "In Cleveland, Ohio, perhaps?"

Ernst responded at this point equally upbeat, "Yes, yes, that's true."

"Would his name be Jack, Jack Miller?" Dad next inquired.

"Yes," Ernst responded, somewhat taken aback.

My father let out a sigh and said, "Well, that's me. How do you do!"

Silence ensued for a full minute. Ernst was so thrilled that he was unable to speak or work. He closed his clothing shop and went directly home to tell his wife, Edith, and wait for my parents to arrive.

It was fifty-two years since he had last seen his younger brother, Ernst. He looked his name up in the Tel Aviv phone book while in Israel on holiday. Simple enough! Yes, Ernst Mueller. Go to the "M's" and there you have it. Indeed, there was a listing.

But I go too fast. There is a reason they weren't in communication all those years. Why? Because Ernst was mad at him. He had asked my father to send him a taxi—yes, you read that correctly, a taxi—and my father refused.

So, you might ask, what brought them together? An early fiftieth wedding anniversary present that brought my parents on a trip to Europe. It was my mother's first trip abroad. My father used to say, "I've been there, you wouldn't like it," in a low, gruff voice. "I want to remember it as it was, not with what happened to it when the Germans made my family house their headquarters. Where I grew up doesn't even exist anymore."

Memories of his childhood included a peaceful estate with a general store, a bar, and a farm with cattle and horses. He didn't care to see what war had done to his past.

He was born in a small village in Austria-Hungary (that was the country's name at the time, what today is the Czech Republic).

Before this trip, I remember saying to my father more than once, "Daddy, don't you have a brother in Israel?" He always answered with the same few words, "Yes, that's right, I sure do."

"How are you going to find him?" I would then inquire.

He always astonished me with: "Oh, I'll find my brother!"

"But how, Daddy?"

"I'll look him up in the phone book," was his consistent reply. And so, he did.

My parents got to Ernst's house without incident or delay. The reunion was very touching. There was hugging, standing back, looking into each other's eyes, comparing their likenesses, and more hugging. After all, fifty-two years!

It was like they were looking in a mirror. Both Ernst and my father had well-manicured hands, large fingernails, flat-surfaced but mooned. They were both Dapper Dans in their haberdashery, down to the polished black shoes and black nylon socks that came halfway up their calves. They had the same smile and pale sea-green eyes, and similarly large ear lobes. They both stood five foot five inches with straight backs, full heads of snow-white hair, and dark complexions. They were both in good physical shape, fit and trim. They each carried themselves in a manner that spoke loudly as if to say, 'Hey, I'm here, notice me, respect me, I'm a person to be reckoned with.'

My mother related this story to me in great detail. I was able to see it as if it were a picture. My mother and Edith were in the background like in an out-of-focus photograph as they watched with broad grins and wet overflowing eyes as their husbands showed a soft side of themselves neither woman had ever seen before. There were no words to describe the depth of their having been touched by being witness to this. Those were the women who kept saying, "I can't believe this is happening. I've never seen my husband like this." And my mother would almost mirror back to Edith, "They are full of wonder and love. Words are not enough here to express the deep-seated connection and love all these years ago and now, seamless as if it were just yesterday they'd been together." The men and the women had their own language to express to each other. Shivers ran through everyone deeply involved and witnessing it at the same time.

I met Ernst on my first trip to Israel, having never seen him before even in any recent photograph. Even though he is a half-brother to my father, the resemblances were there just as my mother had described. He drove me around his city, Tel Aviv, and to his house for a meal and to meet his wife, Edith. My cousin Edith from Haifa who accompanied me on this trip was our translator.

But there was one stop on the way. He took me to his clothing store so I could get souvenir T-shirts for my little children. However, he gave me much more than the T-shirts. I left with two shopping bags full of clothes for myself and my kids, and he wouldn't take any money for this. Edith from Haifa stood by in awe. Anytime she was in the store, he made her pay for the littlest thing!

I don't speak Hebrew and Uncle Ernst doesn't speak English. I understand very little Yiddish or German, so he went slowly, and I talked with my hands, and from my heart, and we understood each other and got along famously.

That day a bond was created between Uncle Ernst and me. Together we speak a language of our own. Our eyes and our touch communicate what is important. That we are related, that we care deeply for one another, and that life is precious. Because he is so close to my father, and I adored my father, I automatically adored my Uncle Ernst. Another one of those 'moments in time' was choreographed better than I could have even imagined. Clearly it was not my doing.

The magic and blessings of this meeting and divine intervention have me filled with gratitude and love.

Ever since then, my parents communicated in writing to Ernst, if nothing more than during the holidays. Whenever Ernst and Edith came to the States, they visited not only my parents in Florida but usually made a stop in New York, and I got to spend time with my uncle and Edith.

Edith, his wife, was fluent in English but she went to the lady's room at one point. We were left alone, without anyone to translate for us. We created a middle language all our own.

Ernst and my father are both gone now but these moments live on in my heart.

Clothing

It was a sunny Springtime Sunday around 11 a.m. in Cleveland. Shadows crept across the driveway from the apple and cherry trees on either side. We were walking briskly and purposefully down the long driveway. Mother, father, and daughter (me) in the middle, holding hands, all dressed in white short-sleeved shirts or blouses with matching beige gabardine slacks custom made to order. It was Sunday and we were going to visit my parents' friends.

My mother, with her straight back and brownish-blonde hair piled on top of her head, looked very much like Barbara Stanwyck. My father, with his full head of black hair except for that one white streak that ran front to back on the left side, could easily pass for a bootlegger, bouncer, or Edward G. Robinson's double. I had long, tight brown braids crisscrossed atop my head held in place in the back with a white ribbon. I had a smile pasted on my face as if the photographer had demanded, "Ok, everyone smile NOW!"

This image is so clear in my mind that even though the snapshot is in black and white, I see the colors. I felt so important and grown up dressed like my mom and dad.

In my childhood, I had all my clothes made until I was out of high school. My father had a men's clothing factory and his supervisor, Angelo, fabricated beautiful velvet jumpers in green, maroon, and black for me. He was a very friendly man, always smiling, and hugged me whenever my father took me with him to work. The factory-made men's slacks and Bermuda shorts, no women's clothes.

I cut out pictures of skirts I liked in magazines or newspapers, and he copied them into skirts for me.

I felt I was different. I wanted to be like the other girls, to go shopping in the stores. It never happened. I was taken to a manufacturer, chose clothes, and prayed they fit because returns were not allowed. In today's world it sounds lovely, but it wasn't lovely to me. It kept me apart from, rather than a part of, the other girls.

The material would come from what was left over from an order. As I got older, my mother would take me to Mr. Petrocelli, the tailor, and he made me skirts in every color. Once I brought a newspaper clipping of a style I liked. I asked Mr. Petrocelli, "Could you make me a skirt with this design?" His response was, "How many do you want?" And I had five skirts made—green, brown, pink, grey, and a speckled blue designed by a man unknown to me at the time, named Evan Picone, a fashion designer.

Because of my father's affiliations and relationships in the clothing industry, he had access to various women's lines. As a result, four times a year I went to the showrooms of what would be the equivalent of Liz Claiborne, Ann Klein, and Bobbie Brooks and chose clothes for each season. I looked at samples, had to guess my size, and then a month to six weeks later, cartons of clothes arrived at our home. I wasn't allowed to complain; nothing could be returned. "You don't do that when people are being kind to you, and you are buying wholesale." That was my father in a stern voice.

In high school I ordered cashmere sweaters from Dalton, not one at a time, but by the dozen. Not because I was spoiled and wanted twelve of them, but because that was the procedure when buying wholesale. Otherwise, it's a nuisance purchase. I still have one from when I was sixteen. It is a short sleeve pink V-neck slipover with grey crocheting around the collar and sleeve edges. My initials, at the time, RAM, are in the corner. It still fits me today and wears like iron. It's a true Laverne and Shirley sweater. This continued until I was out of high school, maybe sixteen or seventeen.

As I write this, I think it's a hoot to have had all these luxuries as a child. But that is in retrospect. In childhood, it made me feel different from everyone else. I already felt that way because my folks were older than everyone else's parents. After all, I had a sister sixteen years older who was married by the time I was in school. All of my friends had at least one brother or sister in close age proximity. For all intents and purposes, I was like an only child.

My friends' parents were all American-born, or so I assumed. I was a child of an immigrant, yet I never felt that way for even one day. I am surprised to even write it here, but it's the truth.

We had two cars in our family, everyone else had one. My father's car was nicer, but my mother's car had personality. When I was out with my friends, my mother was often who picked us up from the roller-skating rink, the movies, or one another's homes. Sixteen years made a difference then and probably would be today in terms of affluence and influence.

Back then I just wanted to be included, to be popular, to have friends, to be like everyone else, to even look and dress like everyone else. I wanted to go shopping in the department stores with my friends. No one had clothes like mine. No one shopped like I did. Everyone else had permission to go to the department stores and use their mother's charge card to buy clothes, as needed, for school. Everyone that is, except me.

Many of my friends had after-school jobs, contributing to the household. Some had to rush home to babysit a younger sibling. I always asked for one. "Mom, can I have a baby sister or brother?" The answer was always in one form or another 'No.'

One odd year I was in search of a winter coat. Both my parents were with me at a department store in the local mall in Cleveland. I found one I loved. My father inspected it and said, "It's not made well; it isn't for you. Let's get going."

"But, Daddy, I really like it. Please? Oh please?" My mother, who never crossed what he said, interrupted with a tone of voice reserved (I thought) only for me, "Oh let her have the darn coat already! There's nothing wrong with it." And you know what? He did. This is the only memory I have of shopping in a department store in my childhood. I was surprised my mother spoke up, and in a public place too.

Today I would be so honored to have my clothes made to fit and in styles I chose. It's all about perception and it feels like the healing is in shifting my perceptions about my past.

When I was a teenager and I'd go to either of my parents for money, I learned early on whom to go to. If I went to my mother, she would give me $5 or $10 and ask for change. When I went to my father, he gave me $20 and never asked for change! Yes, I took full advantage of that. In later years, he was known as 'Lord Tightwad' but not when I was a child. His theory was 'You don't need anything; you just want it." We used to joke that he got a cramp when putting his hand in his pocket.

Regarding credit cards, was it because he was born in Europe and there weren't credit cards in the early 1900s? Was it his strict upbringing? Were these the belief systems at the time? I don't know the answer to any of these questions except maybe the first as my father was born in 1898. I doubt credit cards were around then. But he didn't believe in them. His position was 'You pay for what you want in cash only. Otherwise, you're paying for something long after it is used.'

When he was in his eighties, he got his first credit card and 'used it wisely' (his words) and he always paid in thirty days. That part I agree with, and I don't use installment plans either. I am my father's daughter.

One of my father's beliefs that was instilled in me was you always have to have money in the bank. I remember I had to have $1,000 in the bank before I had my first child. And I did. So maybe my father was right? I have no idea what would or could have happened to me if I hadn't. I expect nothing except for $1,000 less than I have now.

When I got my first job as a teenager, my father gave me two choices. He said, "You can give me your paychecks and I'll pay all your bills, medical, food, etc."

To which I replied loudly, "No! I will not do that!"

He said, "Your second choice is you pay your mother room and board and pay all your own bills." I was shocked. We were not poor and so I said resentfully, with my hands on my hips and wanting to lash out, "I pick choice number two." At that point he told me, "You'll get all the money you paid back when you get married." The jury is still out on that one.

The next issue was I wanted a car. I had a job in a local department store. I was sixteen. In Ohio, you could get a license at sixteen. My father found me a new car. Standing tall, arms crossed across his chest, shoulders back, he proceeded to impart what he considered vital information to me. He lectured, "You buy a used car, you're buying someone else's problems." My father had an opinion on everything, and he was always right. Just ask him. So, it had to be a new car and an American car. Chevrolet was the winner because of the price.

To pay for this new car, he would be my finance company. I had to pay him $100 a month until it was paid for. I agreed, again resentfully.

Financial Fears

When my father was in his seventies, he was always worried about money, and he spoke to me about it for the first time. He had a list he kept on an end table next to his favorite chair of whatever he owned and what his capital amounted to. The paper was worn thin as he used it as a worry stone, I think.

He was genuinely concerned that he'd run out and not be able to support his family. People said (to this day I don't know who 'they' are) that he was undercapitalized. All I knew was he had money invested in the stock market and lost a great deal of it. Money and finances, except for rules about them, weren't discussed in our house.

I was my father's daughter and he taught me very well to worry about money: having it, having enough, spending it, being paralyzed to touch it in any options. That was until one day I changed my mind.

Here's what shifted how I interact with money. My husband Tony was the catalyst. He got fired from his six-figure salary. I thought he was kidding. Standing there in jeans and a golf tee shirt in my favorite color of light green, he said, "Let's go to Italy." At almost the same time, I said, "Are you crazy? We can't do that! I'll get my old job back and we'll sell the new furniture..." He interrupted me with: "When will we ever have three weeks that we can go away together?" I had no response. And we went to Italy.

My father said, "I don't understand how you can do that without a job now. Do you have money in the bank? Never mind, it's none of my business. Have a nice trip." And we did and we lived to tell the story.

Sadly, Tony and I amicably divorced and remained friends until his death.

At one time in my career, I got a wooden plaque, a prestigious acknowledgment of my work. I was with my parents, sharing with them this wonderful achievement. I was so proud of myself, and I was hoping they would be too. And my father interrupted with: "But is there a man in your life?" Not again. I spoke slowly and clearly," Daddy, I am a successful person working a great job and I am able to take care of myself and my children." He backed down a bit, but I was to learn that until I remarried, he felt responsible for me. Gotta love him for that at some level.

Integrity & The $5,000 Gall Bladder

MUCH OF MY FATHER's belief systems are antiquated now, but, in his time and age, they were very important for survival. And being born in Europe he had strong familial rules handed down by his father. The best one is integrity. He role-modeled it for me. He gave his word. He kept his word. He was his word. It sets the bar as to what's acceptable or not in relationships. And I inherited this and it's #1 on my list of principles. I'm very grateful to him for this. I keep my word no matter what. I am my father's daughter.

At the end of his life, he still had that list of what was invested or in the bank, and it did survive him. I choose to believe this allows him to rest in peace. He did what he was taught to do. He was very responsible. He loved his family. He wanted the best for them. He only mellowed later, much later, with the rigidity he attached to some of his beliefs.

My father, a self-made man, took his responsibilities seriously and stood for what he believed in. Sometimes I sense his presence, especially around his birthday, and while my lifestyle is beyond his comprehension, he's leaning on a column, hands folded across his chest, smiling because he is so very proud of me. And for that, I love him.

I held my mother under her arms like human crutches and helped her walk one step at a time until we got to the doorway of my father's hospital room. Then I released her, and on her own volition, she took three steps to dad's bedside. We did the reverse upon exiting and getting her home to rest. No one was the wiser.

My mom was a wreck, projecting what-if's: what if this happens, what if that happens, what will happen to her, what will happen to me, and so on. She was useless. Her legs were wobbly, and she appeared weak and fragile. The medication she was on had her constantly burping. A family joke was if we couldn't find her, just follow the burps.

The backstory is he was complaining of heartburn and my mother wanted him to go to the ER which happened to be just up the road from their apartment. He said no. He never liked doctors and said it was probably indigestion and it would pass. She insisted that he go and to quiet her, he went. He had symptoms of a heart attack, and they were handling him as if it were so. It was not accurate.

By the time they realized it was his gall bladder, he was almost too weak to be operated on. They did, however, remove his gall bladder successfully.

I am in Florida yet again. My sister strongly urged that I come, and she ended with, "Bring your kids. This may be a long visit."

She also suggested I don't see him right after the operation. If he were to see me, he might think he was dying. Too bad, I wanted to see my dad. I was there when he came back to his room. I was afraid to look, scared of what I might see, worried about what might show on my face. What a surprise. He looked terrific, with rosy cheeks, peaceful, and rested. Later I was to find out he had a blood transfusion and that's why he looked so good.

I then went into operation (no pun intended). I arranged for round-the-clock nurses at the hospital. Dad was in a private room rather than intensive care—for psychological reasons I was told. I found nurses, set their schedules, contacted the doctor in charge, and handled whatever contingencies arose. After all, I'm the businessperson in the family (well-trained by my dad, I might add).

The hospital was on the corner of the street where my parents lived. My kids and I walked to the northernmost corner of the catwalk of their building at a designated time, and the nurse brought my father to the window of the hospital by its fire door, and we could almost see him and vice versa. We took this daily trek and waved and waved. The nurse saw us and had him wave back.

The good news was he was recuperating ahead of schedule. His vanity was such that he insisted on a haircut because he felt so scruffy. He obtained permission from the doctor to leave the hospital with the nurse, get picked up by me, driven to and from a haircut, and then returned to the hospital. He was much more exhausted than he anticipated, but he did have his hair cut.

Once home, we took care of him. Mother was a little more useful, seeing that he really did survive this operation. However, she was squeamish around wounds, so I was the 'elected' nurse to change the bandages and help him dress and undress. He was a very private man who never let anyone do anything for him. But he let me help him.

My children kept him occupied during the day and were ever so careful to stay away from his tender left hand—the arm the intravenous was in. It was bruised black, blue, orange, and green and hurt him a great deal.

After five days of his being home from the hospital, I had to return to New York to close on my family's home on Long Island. It wasn't supposed to happen for several weeks, but stuff happens, that's life.

The night before I left, my mom and I were sitting on the couch making small talk conversation, facing the TV, not each other. Suddenly, she put her arm around me and quietly said, "You know, you're my security blanket. Now that you're leaving, I don't know what I'll do. I mean, I know we'll be fine, but I'm going to really miss you." Then she hugged me tightly.

Was this my mother? The one I usually talk and write about? I was speechless. My eyes spilled over with buckets of tears. My mom really knew how to get to me. I felt so important, so needed, so acknowledged, so loved. It was wonderful.

When my dad heard I was leaving, he also floored me. "I promised to loan you $5,000 towards your house and I am keeping my word. Before I had this operation, we had an agreement." He proceeded to tell me which bank to withdraw the money from, which bank to deposit it into, and where his checkbook was. Before I left, I had in hand the check for $5,000.

The bonus was being able to support my mother and have her acknowledge it.

It's almost forty years later and it's such a fond memory, and most likely another one of those lessons for me in which I learned that when all was said and done, all I have is my word.

Mixed Messages

I was a good girl and I wanted to get a "good girl" from each of my parents. However, what I got praised for one day I got punished for the next. Mixed messages were rampant. My father was such a tyrant, so scary and cruel, I'm surprised I am alive today. When he was in one of his moods, he was another person and couldn't hear a word I said. I learned to walk on eggs carefully, making myself invisible tiptoeing around to not upset the applecart.

I didn't say much because one doesn't talk back to a parent. That's disrespectful, but it only went one way. I wasn't entitled to respect. His favorite one-liner was: "If it weren't for me, you wouldn't be here!" I never knew what that meant but it sounded ominous the way he said it, so I got back on my eggshells.

The one I remember the most is, "You can be or do anything you want, anything you set your mind to." my mother said this repeatedly.

On the other hand, she also said, 'You'll never amount to anything. Why can't you be more like your sister?" Another favorite missive to me.

I remember as a young girl I wanted to take ballet and she said, "You can't do ballet. You're a klutz. You can take tap dancing." And I did. And I hated it.

I was an overachiever with low self-esteem. I learned to zip up and stay in my head which was safer, rather than going into my heart where I could get 'murdalized'--my childhood word for fear. This became my survival method. I was a 'human doing' rather than a 'human being' for the better part of my life.

These mixed messages reminded me of the game show *Who Do You Trust?* Door #1, Door #2, or Door #3. However, blood is thicker than water, so any compliments were taken with a grain of salt. Mother really knew best, right? I can hear her saying, while nodding her head, "Other people tell you what you want to hear, but you can always trust Mother."

When I was in elementary school, my mother found a piece of paper on the steps containing a list of curse words. I had put it there to take upstairs and forgot to do it. I wrote them down so I would remember them. She called me into the living room and defined each of the words. She chastised me for not coming to her to ask their meaning.

Then she said, "Tell me who told you or wrote these down for you. Nothing will happen, just tell me the truth." I proceeded to tell her, "Janet from up the block." She interrupted me before I could say another word. "I don't want you playing with that girl anymore! You understand?"

My subdued response was, "Yes, Mother."

When I was in junior high school, I talked back to my mother and was sent to my room and was grounded by my father. I very much wanted to go to the junior prom and that meant asking my father if I could be set free from being grounded in my room. I rehearsed my request a dozen times and came to the top of the stairs. With a deep breath, I began my slow descent. Midway down, I did an about-face and ran back up. The risk was too high to get him mad or extend the punishment. I went back to my room with my tail between my legs. My fear was bigger than my desire. I never got to the prom that year.

The Attic

Huge colorful movie placards, like the kind theaters advertise their current or coming attractions, wallpapered the slanted walls. *Pennies from Heaven* and other unknown-to-me titles with movie stars like Norma Shearer, also unknown to me, were all around. "Mom, who are these people and why do we even have these?" "Your uncle, my brother Jack, was in business in California and would periodically send them to me. They're all from before you were born. They're advertising the upcoming movies in local theatres."

On one side of the attic, balanced on the eaves, were games—Tiddlywinks, Parcheesi, Pick-Up Sticks, and Dominos. My favorite was Pick-Up Sticks. I don't remember how to play the others. The wooden shoes were gathering dust. I took them to show-and-tell in second grade. I told my class: "These are from Holland. My cousin Arthur bought them just for me when he was in the Navy."

Next there was my amazing stamp collection. Four albums reflected the time, love, and energy that went into my collecting, locating the proper country and stamp, licking and attaching the hinges, and affixing the stamps. I spent hours matching stamps and learning the names of countries I couldn't even pronounce. I always believed I had stamps that were rare and very valuable. My favorites, big and colorful ones, were from Nicaragua and Ceylon. Now they're just a memory.

Why? My father, unbeknownst to me, hired a liquidator who came into the house and sold everything that wasn't nailed down. We were downsizing and moving from my house, the only one I ever knew, to an apartment. I was in my second year of college.

"Dad, where is my stamp collection? It was right here last time I was home." He calmly said, "It was sold." My shoes were sold, two pairs for a dollar. My roller skates went for fifty cents a pair. Tiddlywinks was a memory. Pick-Up Sticks were nonexistent. "And all of my comic books, where are they?" There wasn't one to be found. His response was, "Gone, sold. They're all gone."

I felt invisible, disregarded, and disrespected by my father. His response was, "Stop whining, you didn't use it anyhow." And when he was mad, his typical line was, "If it weren't for me, you wouldn't be here." I suppose that is true, really true, but it still hurt. I felt like I didn't matter and there was no respect for what was mine. It all was my father's to do with as he wished. It was the Golden Rule, again, he who has the gold makes the rules. That was my father.

Then there were the famous and memorable dolls that were an exact replica of the civil marriage ceremony in Czechoslovakia, brought to America by my father in the early 1900s. I wasn't allowed to play with them. "These aren't toys, after all, but you can look at them." And I did, often. They were each about three feet in height. The man's authentic black leather boots even had heels. The woman had a fancy headdress and an accordion-pleated back to her dress. The front was ornate and colorful brocade with multicolored sequins sewn on. The dolls were kept in a large box amidst lots of tissue paper. And they still are, in my closet in a large box amidst lots of tissue paper. These were the only keepsakes saved because they were considered a family heirloom and maybe worth money. They had no markings or labels to research how much they were worth.

My sister's wedding dress was neatly folded in a large white box with tissue paper all around. There were so many little buttons all the way down the back of the dress. I couldn't figure out how she got it on and off.

In the wintertime, the attic was very cold and as inert as ice. You could see your breath. It fogged up the small triangular windows at each end of the room. In the summer it was hot, stale, musty, and stuffy; the air never moved or circulated. Yet it held such fascination for me. It was like going into another dimension. It was so quiet and full of history and had my special things there for safekeeping, or so I thought. I would lovingly and gently check on the dolls, reread my comics, and sometimes, unbeknownst to anyone, try on my sister's wedding dress with all the buttons down the back.

It's been many years, maybe thirty-five years later, and I still have the dolls. Because there are no markings on them, we don't know whether they are worth $30 or $3,000. Or if the story is even true.

'I wonder if he'd have sold me if I were there, I thought sarcastically to myself. Was the money more important than me? All the things were not only mine, but they represented my childhood and my happy memories. And I had no say in the matter. He could have told me, "Someone is coming to sell the stuff in the attic, take what you want and put it in the second bedroom, or it'll be gone." But he didn't. He could have put what was clearly mine in a carton and set it aside for me. Nope.

He relentlessly drilled into me I had no rights, was utterly undeserving of respect, and had no permission to talk about his or my mothers' friends. I never liked those people who, when they saw me, pinched my cheeks. Once I made the mistake of speaking up about it. I hated when people did that to me. That was when I learned my lesson to keep quiet, don't make waves, just obey. It was clear I had no rights.

I was very hurt and, behind that or maybe in front of it, angry, actually full of rage. But good girls don't get angry, nor do they talk back to their fathers. And so, I stuffed it. Many years later I have the opportunity to see where these emotions exist in my life in today's world. I have more tools and choices to deal with them today, instead of just bottling them up.

I have made peace with my father, though in all honesty if he were alive, he could still trigger my negative feelings. My first husband was one of his representatives to show me I need more healing. My ex could push my buttons faster than choosing a song on the jukebox. B-3 was Invisible You; G-2 was Me and My Anger, D-4 was How Low Can You Go (self-esteem). And then as I processed and grew up, A-7 played The Book of Love (self-love) and erased all the other records. I was back in the present without having someone else choose who I was and what I did or did not feel. It was safe to express my feelings. Writing this story brought up a similar incident many years later, but that's the next story.

Oh No! Not Again!

MY MIND IS RACING with: 'I cannot believe this. It's happened again. Why can't I have what is mine; why do I keep being ripped off? Why am I not considered important enough to be asked, to be appreciated, to be deserving of common courtesy and participation in the results? Am I still invisible, do I matter not? He can do whatever he wants with what is or is not his?'

I know he believes this to be true. He makes the rules, it's his house, and he can do whatever he wants. But enough is enough!

To my father, I said as calmly as my inside screamer would allow, "Where is the gold-on-gold China that my mom specifically left to me? It was right here in the breakfront. Where is it now? Did you move it? It's mine, where is it?" The level of my inquiry now had a shrill high-pitched sound. I was doing my best not to throw something or burst into tears.

My father quietly said, "I sold it." "How could you do that; it was willed to me. How dare you! I loved it and Mom knew it which is why she willed it to me." I had never spoken to my father like that but look what he'd done. This has got to stop.

I went through the breakfront a dozen times, double-checking, triple-checking, and nothing. These were gold-on-gold-designed serving pieces. I can picture the soup tureen with a very dainty cover, large, handled bowls, all with this beautiful gold-on-gold shimmering with love from my mother, used for special occasions had wonderful loving memories for me. When we had company only good dishes and silverware were used. My mother also said "Be sure to put the salt and pepper shakers at the far end of the table, closest to where your father sits. He will use them first and pass them to our guests." And they were gone. Not even one. And he did it without asking me if I wanted it, just thinking of himself and the money he could get for them.

As it happened, the glass doors to the breakfront had a wooden strip holding their closures. Behind this two-inch strip of wood were the gold-on-gold salt and pepper shakers. They were small, maybe two inches high, but I was so excited.

This was the last of what my mother wanted me to have. And I loved them as much as she did. She even wrote a codicil to her will specifically repeating that "Al the gold-on-gold goes to my daughter, Rosanne." You can't be any clearer than that.

I loved these salt and pepper shakers so much, I would go to the breakfront, open the door, reach behind, and take them out and hold them, really caressing them in my hand, closing my fingers over them, and imagining my mother using them. I can hear her saying, "Pass the salt and pepper shakers, please." They were for company, of course, but my mother was a great cook and so they had a lot of mileage. As I held them in one hand and then the other, I could feel my mother's energy placing them just so on the dining room table. They weren't smooth to the touch, so I pretended I could feel the gold on them. When I came back to the present moment, I carefully put them back where my father couldn't get near them.

I was so mad at my father that I wouldn't speak to him. Every Sunday at 5 p.m. he called from Florida to my house in NY. My husband, Tony, would answer and hold the receiver towards me with: "Come on, Ro, it's your father." My response was, "Nope. If he dies, he dies. But I can't forgive this one. His life is behind him. My life is ahead of me." That was the last straw for me. I couldn't find it inside me to let it go as I had almost everything else that he had or had not done.

The backstory here is that there are bad people in the world who read obituaries and look for a lone-surviving next-of-kin and come knocking on the door. They assume, rightly so in our case, that my father was angry, thrown, so very sad that one day my mother was there and two days later she was dead. These people come to the door and see if they can buy what is in the breakfront. They took advantage of my father, and he always had a love relationship with money, so he sold all the 'good stuff.' These people were, of course, untraceable as was our China.

I didn't speak to my father. Tony spoke to him but I was done. This went on for weeks. Each Sunday at 5:00 p.m. the phone would ring and Tony would answer. He'd once again hold the receiver out to me with raised eyebrows which I interpret as 'please take the call. He's your father. Talk to him. I don't know what to say or do here."

And then one day months later when he called, he was so full of remorse, apologetic, and sad. He kept saying, "Dolly (his childhood name for me), I am so sorry; I wasn't in my right mind. I didn't mean to hurt you. I love you."

It melted the ice around my heart, and I spoke to him. It was like the statute of limitations was up. He cried and, through his tears, said, "I am so sorry. Please forgive me. I was crazed then and angry that she left me. I am so sorry for what I did. I didn't mean to hurt you. I love you. You're my Dolly."

I forgave him and I forgave myself for having to put him through that. It wasn't his intention to offend or insult me; he was a man mourning the sudden loss of his partner whom he had been with for sixty-six years. I could be the bigger person. And in forgiving him I healed something in myself as well.

At the same time, I gave myself a pat on the back for standing up for my feelings for once, even when it was about my father. The gift for me here was the process of forgiveness. I wasn't ready until I was ready.

In doing so, I felt peaceful and in a deeper and more authentic relationship with my father and with myself. There were no longer those voices in my head debating what I should or should not do, and/or when or if I should do it.

The physical gift for me is I do have salt and pepper shakers which represent a precious part of my relationship with my mother.

Adulthood & New York

WHEN I WAS TWENTY-THREE, we moved to Florida. I was brought up to believe that good girls lived at home until they were married. However, I didn't like Florida. I went to New York on a vacation and visited two friends from Cleveland who had moved there. They both worked so I took a part-time job to fill my days. I was on a $90 round-trip fare and kept extending my return because I had money from working and a place to stay.

I loved New York and always wanted to live there. Our arrangement was I could stay with them and in exchange for no rent, I would clean and cook. This was OK by me.

I did return to Florida about eight or nine months later, but I was discontented and missed my friends. I moved to New York to the horror of my parents. "You have until April (it was November at the time) to come back. That's when our lease is up." They would then move into a one-bedroom instead of remaining in their present two-bedroom. Their neighbors, as well as friends of mine, thought I'd be disowned, but that didn't happen. And my parents never moved either.

Apartment hunting in New York City presented a real challenge for me. Over the phone, the apartment as described sounded perfect. One bedroom, small eat-in kitchen, living/dining room combination, air conditioning, elevator building, tree-lined street, and in my price range. However, upon arrival, the agent showed me a rinky-dink efficiency, nothing like what was discussed or described over the phone.

Having just arrived from Florida with one of my great summer tans, brown as a bunny, this agent made mother right. I was too dark. Therefore, they would not rent to me, assuming my ethnic background to be other than it was.

I lived in New York for over fifty years in a refurbished studio apartment on the upper East Side on Eighty-first Street between First and Second Avenue. When my father found out the location, he smiled and said, "When I lived in New York I was on Eighty-third between First and Second." Small world or coincidence?

In 2007 I moved to Northern Virginia to be near my daughter, and this is where I am staying.

Atlanta & Belgium Waffles

THE WHITE STRETCH LIMO waited for us outside the hotel. Mom, in her inimitable Barbara Stanwick walk, preceded us out the door. My father was still going over what he saw. "I can't believe all that you did. Where did you learn this? I loved being there with you and seeing the respect all the people showed you. What an amazing job you did." My mom nodded and proceeded to seat herself in the limo through the open door.

My father and I then got in and, without realizing it, didn't use the same door as Mom and found ourselves in a row in front of her. "So, this is what they mean by a s-t-r-e-t-c-h limo," I said. We all had a good laugh. She stayed put and Dad and I stayed where we were, and we left for the airport. This was the first time in twenty-five years we had flown together. My folks were coming to New York with me for a visit.

But I'm ahead of myself. We're leaving and we haven't arrived yet.

At this point in time, I'm a producer of trade shows and this one happened to be in Atlanta, the closest I've ever come on business to Florida where my folks lived. I invited them to 'come on up and see me' and see what I do firsthand. "We can all travel together to New York then." I more than invited them. I offered free tickets, free transportation to and from the airport, free room, meals, the whole enchilada. I made them an irresistible offer they couldn't refuse. And they didn't.

Being busy with the setup, I sent the hotel car to pick them up at the airport and worked until they arrived. This was such an incredible treat for me. Yes, they had been to my office in New York City on trips north, but in my new position having them witness what I did was a dream come true for me.

They settled into their room and came to the evening's opening cocktail party. They arrived as I was welcoming people from the stage over the microphone. The audience included exhibitors for the trade show—hoteliers and resort personnel who traveled extensively. I interrupted myself and said, "Everyone, please notice the short man with the white hair walking towards the stage area, well that's my dad. And the lady sitting at the table closest to the podium, well that's my mom. Be sure and stop by and say hello."

Having produced these trade shows for about ten years, I was friendly with most of the exhibitors, enough at least for them to know I had two parents. None of these people, however, had met either one of them.

People came to them in droves. Those who hadn't been in touch of late with their own folks made up for it with mine. Lots of people spoke highly of me, which my dad and my mom just loved (and me too).

After the cocktail party it was my responsibility to supervise the configuration of the trade show, a pipe-and-drape setup. However, the main ballroom was in use. Pat Boone was performing for a private organization. At midnight mom went to bed, but my dad stayed up well past his bedtime with me. He loved being in the middle of things.

He kept saying to anyone who would listen, "I'm just so amazed. I don't know where she learned all this. I think it's just terrific," as he was leaning against one of the columns outside the main ballroom with his arms crossed across his chest. He was so honored to be included and to witness what he had only heard at one time or another.

The next day at the luncheon I sat them at a table up front so they could hear the guest speaker. To my chagrin, I looked over and found them both dozing. I quickly looked to see if my boss noticed, and I needn't have concerned myself. He, too, was dozing!

At the closing cocktail party so many people came over to say goodbye to my folks. My parents evoked some of the unsaid communication, the rushed telephone calls, the overdue visits that each person felt in relation to their own parents.

But that's not the end of this story...

The next morning before departing, we had breakfast at the hotel. For the first time ever in his eighty-some years, my father tasted a Belgian waffle. And, I might add, he loved it. He was always a picky eater, eating only American food that he could see. For instance, a steak, a baked potato and green beans (not from a can). He never tasted anything outside his regular diet or ate stews or casseroles.

However, by virtue of his trust in his daughter, me, he was willing to try the Belgian waffle. With strawberries and whipped cream, of course, and he loved it. "I can't believe how good this is. I never had one before, it's amazing. Don't even ask. I'm not sharing. Get your own." It was the one and only time he ever had one.

As I replay this scenario, it hits me what a gift it was for my parents to be there with and for me. I'm not sure who loved it more, them or me. I think it was me. There was a confident, competent person introduced to them that no amount of conversation could accomplish yet their fresh eyes could see. I'm blessed to have given them a bird's eye view of what my work encompassed. I'm also seeing it through their eyes, and I do get the respect given to me and it gets added to my own self-respect.

The Mustache Man

WHEN I WAS YOUNG, whenever I would tell my father about someone I met, or somewhere I was traveling to, he would tell me, "I know someone from there. They have a mustache and wear glasses." It became a running joke in our house that my father knew people everywhere.

On my first honeymoon to St. Croix, Dad again told me he knew someone there. I didn't believe him, and we had a good laugh about it. After all, my father had never been outside of the US once he landed there in the early 1900s. I said, "No more kidding around." Yet he said, "I really do know someone from there. He does wear glasses and has a mustache!"

The honeymoon was prepaid, so we needed only a small amount of cash. We ended up buying Wedgewood China and cut crystal and, of course, needed more money. Skeptical and despite ourselves, we sought the man my father said he knew, Joe, and, lo and behold, we found him. What a surprise. He was real, he did have a mustache, and he did wear glasses. He took us to his bank, vouched for us, and we cashed a check with his help. Amazing.

My father and Joe met when my father was a traveling salesman and Joe worked in a man's clothing store that my father sold men's trousers to. What a small world.

Ominous Phone Call

THEN ONE SUNDAY THE phone rang at 3:30 p.m. Oh no, I thought, something was wrong. It was my father. He said, "You need to come. Your mother wants to see you before she dies." I could barely speak. I found my voice and said, "I'll be on the next plane." Tony asked, "What is wrong with her?" "I don't know," I replied. "It doesn't matter, she wants to see me. She is my mother, so I am going." I was a very responsible sixty-six-year-old daughter.

I was brought up to respect, honor, and obey my parents, regardless of age. There wasn't a second thought of 'should I go?' 'Is it serious?' No, this was my mother and she wanted me there.

When I got there, my father explained, "She went to the doctor on Thursday, and he said her blood pressure was high, which is a forerunner to a stroke." I could have killed the doctor. Hadn't he read her history? Everyone in her family died of a stroke. My father tried to calm her down and finally, by Sunday, he could do no more. Thus, the call for me. My sister lived thirty minutes away but that wouldn't do. The cavalry, me, was beckoned and I immediately complied.

I felt good that I could be there for mom, and she appreciated it as well. I took her to a battery of doctors while I was there to reduce her fears, and she lived many years after that. She did get scared because of the insensitivity of the doctors in Florida.

Three Generations

"Three Generations and Two World Wars" read the front page of the *Miami Herald* on March 1, 1988. The article began: "In Broward (the county) the reunion of three lifetimes..." The newspaper's picture showed my father walking towards two women, my mother off to his left, and everyone smiling from ear to ear. Then the embrace. "Oh, my goodness, I can't believe this is happening. It's an absolute miracle!"

In the summer of 1987, my father found that his sisters were in Australia. My father's half-brother Ernst in Israel was in touch with Hermina and Elizabeth, and he assumed my father knew of them and their whereabouts. However, it never came up in conversation.

He got their contact information from Ernst and wrote them a letter, telling them who he was and wanting to hear from them as soon as possible. He waited and waited, very impatiently, I might add. Almost six months passed before he finally got a reply. Why? Because they had been traveling but as soon as they got the letter, they responded and then planned a trip to the United States.

It had been seventy-four years since my father was reunited with his sisters he had previously thought dead. They came all the way from Melbourne, Australia, to Hallandale, Florida. Hermina, eighty, a widow, and the older sister, remembered when she was six years old and her brother Jack, (my dad) who was a teenager at the time, had left to come to America. She reminisced, "I was so proud of him. I still remember his standing tall in his blue bell-bottom trousers." Elizabeth, his baby sister, had not yet been born.

They spoke English, so communication was not a problem. They were open, loving, and so happy to be with family. Watching my dad interact with these newfound sisters was a delight. He couldn't pass them in a room without reaching out to touch an arm, a hand, a face, and always ever so gently with a smile. There was a softness about him I had never seen before.

Daily, he would declare, "Isn't this a miracle? Aren't they nice? Isn't this something?" For someone who was a constant conversationalist, they had him at a loss for words.

There was childlike amazement on their faces to be together after all those years. In the case of Elizabeth, to first meet and instantly love her older brother was a gift. Words weren't adequate. Looks and touches said it all and were felt by everyone in the room. It truly was a miracle.

They told us stories upon stories of their youth before and after the war. Elizabeth had survived a concentration camp; Hermina was hired out as a maid in private employ to wait out the war. They were not angry but grateful to be alive.

If this weren't occasion enough, it was my parents' sixty-fifth wedding anniversary also. The entire family, albeit our tiny family, was present for both auspicious occasions.

My father had arranged for his sisters to stay in an empty apartment at their condominium complex so they could be nearby.

One night Elizabeth's husband called my father's house, but she had already gone home to go to bed. I asked my son, Kevin, to run downstairs and get her for the call. He wouldn't go. He said, "I'm not banging on a door and calling her name, not in the middle of the night, not after she had been in a concentration camp, no way." That made sense to me. I wouldn't do it either. His sensitivity at the young age of nineteen made me proud. What did we do? We told Sam, her husband, that he would have to call at another time.

When my immediate family left for New York, the parting for me was so tender and gratifying. To have met these two wonderful, courageous women and to share in the rekindling of the love of family and brother and sister and aunts, my heart was open, and my love barrel was full. I felt like I was in the Jerry Lewis Telethon and my cup runneth over. Our hugs and goodbyes were tearful, joyous for the memories created, and fearful for the unknown future.

I felt privileged to have met my aunts and via correspondence to know my Uncle Sam, Elizabeth's husband. Elizabeth has since passed away, and then Hermina, in failing health, soon followed. The tender memories live on and were re-experienced in this story.

It was such a long time ago and yet I can smile as I write this for the tenderness and joy I saw on my father's face as he reunited with his family. He had a softness unknown to me and yet so authentic you couldn't stop yourself from feeling it too. What a gift to witness and experience in my lifetime. And my children who were teenagers shared in this as well.

87th Birthday Dinner

WE WERE ON THE way home from dinner. Tony, my husband, was driving, and I was next to him in the front seat. My mother and my father were sitting in the back quietly moving their heads from side to side admiring the views. There were only the sounds of evening, horns tooting, music playing from other cars, the sound of the cars accelerating when the lights changed.

I glanced over at Tony, wondering if I should even ask the question on my mind. As it was bubbling up in me with some trepidation, I asked, innocently enough, "Did you have a good time, Daddy? Did you enjoy your dinner?" And my voice was loud as he is hard of hearing. Knowing my parents as I did, I knew my sister's choice of restaurant was a poor one. Dad didn't like buffets, he liked to be served.

Without missing a beat, my father proceeded with, "I must be honest with you. It wasn't very good, the place, the food," and I didn't hear the rest. I was so enraged. I felt my blood boil, the heat rushing to my face, anger filling every cell in my body, and I said through gritted teeth, "You'd think you'd appreciate what we were trying to do for you. After all, it's your eighty-seventh birthday and this restaurant wasn't cheap." The remainder of the drive home was extremely uncomfortable.

Two things you need to know at this point. First, my sister was in charge of choosing the place and she didn't make a good choice. She was our best option, though, as she lived in a nearby town in Florida.

Secondly, when we arrived home, Tony and my father walked ahead of us into the house. Just as mother and I were about to enter through the kitchen, she took me aside and covertly whispered, "Don't pay any attention to him. He's an old man now." I was struck speechless. My mouth dropped open in shock as my brain tried to catch up to what I was hearing. My eyes welled up with tears, and unable to speak I mouthed, Thank you. We proceeded into the house together, also through the kitchen, a bond sweetened by this shared moment.

The third thing is, after we were home maybe five minutes after having offloaded the takeaways from the restaurant and our jackets, my father came to me, uncoached by my mother, I might add, and said, "I'm sorry if I hurt your feelings, I didn't mean to." He should have stopped there. However, he continued to go down that same tunnel where there was no cheese and said, "It really was a bad meal and a poor choice." I honestly don't know what else he said because at that point I tuned him out.

The truth is I didn't have the time or the familiarity to choose Florida restaurants. My older (and only) sister had lived there for many years, so I left it to her. My bad. Now to be clear, my sister isn't a child, she is sixteen years older than me—that's another story—but she likes those early bird restaurants with buffets and that's not my parents' style. And it's my feeling she knew that and proceeded anyway, being guided by money, as even the buffet dinners were expensive. However, if my sister hadn't chosen the venue, the conversation with each of my parents, which I now hold sacred, special, and spiritual, wouldn't have occurred.

The fact that he apologized to me meant the world to me, that he didn't do it perfectly matters not, he did it. I was probably in my fifties at the time, and I can't recall it ever happening before. The same has to be repeated again that my mother never responded supportively like that before either. It's quite possible I owe my father an apology as I had no space for him to give me anything but a thank-you, not a restaurant review that was not to his liking. He was being honest, and it wasn't what I was expecting, both his honesty and my knee-jerk reaction.

Apologies

"I'M SO SORRY, I didn't know any better. It's what I was taught by my father. It's how I was brought up. Can you ever forgive me?" This was coming from my father's mouth. I never thought I'd hear those words from him.

He was so sincere and teary-eyed as he held my two hands in his, kept eye contact, and apologized again and again. At that moment, it melted away all the beatings, smacks, slaps, and spankings I got from that day backward over time. It felt so good to speak to it, to get it out in the open, and to clean it up so that we could go forward in peace and love.

It was a moment frozen in time for me. I'd gotten up early that morning to have a conversation with my father before my mother woke. So, at 6:30 a.m., I was at the kitchen table sitting catty-corner from my father, maybe three inches away from his face. He was wearing a white-on-white short-sleeve monogrammed dress shirt with a pair of Bermuda shorts. I was in my bathing suit and cover-up. I started the conversation. My voice was hesitant, a little broken as part of me was so scared, but the other part was committed to going for the gold, to have this completion in my life, to veto or cancel the story I had been carrying around and believing for years.

And so I began, "Daddy, I want to talk to you about my childhood and how you treated me." I had his full attention now. (Whew, breathe, Rosanne.) "I hated you when I was a kid and feared you at the same time. You beat me and when, not if, I cried, you beat me harder. Today

I know no child deserves to be beaten, don't you agree?" Now he agrees with me. "Of course not," he says, "but I didn't know any better. It was the generation of punishment and spanking. And you're right, no child deserves to be beaten," he repeated. He took off his glasses, as they were all fogged up from the tears rolling down his cheeks.

I continued, "Well I thought I deserved it, and it wasn't until I spoke it out loud that I learned no child deserves to be beaten, me included." I was reliving my childhood memory of following him up the stairs to the hallway between the two bedrooms (where there were no windows, of course) and the ritual beginning. He took off his belt and I stood waiting, eyes down, arms at my side, tears quietly falling down my face and getting absorbed in the carpet. *Whack, whack, whack.* As I write I hear it loud and clear. How powerless I felt, how I knew if I cried, he'd hit me harder. And it hurt and I did cry, and he did beat me harder and that was the ritual in a nutshell.

I don't know what happened next in any of these scenarios. I didn't get beaten often, only when I was so bad I deserved it. This was my contaminated thinking. And looking back, I was a good girl. I never drank, never did drugs, never stole, never was in jail, and the list goes on.

My relationship with my father changed from that day forward. First and foremost, he never laid a hand or belt on me again. Truth be told, I was in my late forties, and it'd been years since he used the belt on me.

There was now a bond between us that only we shared. I experienced freedom from thinking there was a part of me that was a 'bad girl' and I 'deserved to be beaten.' He experienced freedom from passing on what was passed on to him. Now there was only love from father to daughter and vice versa.

90th Birthday Dinner

IT'S NOW TIME TO celebrate my father's ninetieth birthday. As we were preparing to go to dinner, he stopped me in the hallway and said, "Dolly, you're not going to lose any more weight, are you?" Quite a compliment to me. That was the first time he ever mentioned my weight to me. Then my mother said, as I walked into the living room, "How long are you going to keep it off for this time?" Ouch again.

Learning from history, I chose the steak house restaurant near their condo, Manero's, and, of course, he was delighted and thoroughly enjoyed the whole evening. And we were five minutes away. The restaurant put 'Happy Birthday Jack' on their lit outdoor billboard so not only my father and family could see it, but every passerby and hopefully some of his friends. We were all smiling as if the world was celebrating his birthday with us.

I always believed I was his favorite. At least he made me feel that way. In Anne Lamott's book *Bird by Bird*, she talks about her father, and it rings true for me:

"He'd almost always be happy to see me. He could make me feel great. It's so different having a living father who loves you, even someone complex and imperfect. After your father dies, defeat becomes pretty defeating. When he's still alive, there are setbacks and heartbreak, but you're still the apple of someone's eye."[1]

1. Annie Lamott, *Bird by Bird*, Knoph Doubleday Publishing Group 2007, p 22

His Last Car

My mind was racing as the four of us walked to the car. It was what my father called his last car, a boring grey Cadillac which meant so much to him as if he had 'arrived' in life. He had a great sense of humor, especially in his later years. We once had a serious conversation about whether he should get a new car—for his last car—and he decided not to. Why? Because he was in his nineties and said, "Who would give me a five-year loan? Forget about it!"

The Bowling Alley

I WAS WALKING AS fast as I could, excited beyond belief. I had just flown from New York to Florida and went directly to the bowling alley to surprise my mother. I was dressed neatly in a black skirt, cream-colored silk blouse, a burgundy velvet blazer, and a scarf that was under the collar and the lapels of my jacket, a paisley design that matched everything I was wearing. I had on mid-size black high heels and a short gold chain necklace. I remember it as if it were yesterday. It wasn't. It was maybe forty years ago.

I was looking left and right for my mom when she walked straight past me, as if I were invisible.

I screamed, "Mom! Hi, Mom, it's me!" Her response was not what I expected. "Well, I didn't recognize you. You look nice." Ouch. That went directly to the quick.

Be careful what your expectations are, they set you up for disappointment. I thought this time she'd be happy to see me, grab me into a full-body hug, kiss me on one cheek and then the other to make sure I was real. Well, none of the expected, anticipated, or hoped-for happened.

I don't remember anything after that, where we went, if we went together, how long I stayed.

But what I do remember is the sting of her response to seeing me. I was an adult at the time and thought myself put together rather well—I had a great role model in my mom for that. But it wasn't enough. It was never enough. I was never enough.

I'm hoping the statute of limitations, if there were one, was up to how long I was going to carry this around with me. I am an adult, a senior citizen, and yet, I hang onto these one-liners—yes, there were quite a few—as if they were the G-d's honest truth. First off, it's not the truth, it's her opinion—two different things and she's entitled to her opinion. It's what I do with it when it lands on me that matters.

I've held on to it too long! It's time. Today's the day I give it up. And I released her from the position I'd put her in, the category I'd put her in, and for making her the 'bad guy' all these many years.

Perhaps I just caught her off guard at the bowling alley and she didn't know what to say. Maybe she was in deep thought and didn't see anyone as she was walking. Maybe (for sure) it was her way of giving me a compliment, albeit a half-assed one. She did the best she could as a mother, and I took it personally!

But I am no longer a child and can have compassion for a woman who had me in her fortieth year (unheard of back in the 1940s). At some level it was embarrassing for my sixteen-year-old sister. She would push me in my baby carriage and people would think it was her child. And some people made up a story that had her having this baby out of wedlock. Then there were times I'm sure when she felt left out or even competitive as I was the apple of my father's eye.

Deaf is Fine

As our plane smoothly lands in Ft. Lauderdale in the year 1994, I turn to Tony and muse, "I wonder what is on his list this time. It seems every time we come to Florida to visit; my dad has a prepared list of miscellaneous things for us to do for him." I'm not really complaining, he does need help in some areas.

Tony and I agreed this trip was a visit, not a vacation. A vacation is when we go somewhere and enjoy ourselves and it's usually restful and calm. A visit means relatives and somehow we get involved, and then there are time-consuming chores to be done, and peaceful it's not.

"Well, we're here. Let's go find Daddy outside. Remember, he's easy to locate--the white car that looks like it's driving itself." Why? Because my father is about five foot six and he looks through the steering wheel, rather than over it. "See, I told you. Look, there he is."

I ran around to the driver's side and helped Daddy out. We hug and kiss and our free-flowing tears mingle, no words are necessary. It is a tender moment where our hearts are open and sacredly connected. I felt like we were moving slowly as if in a movie. Everything around us stood still or moved in slow motion. There was only me and my father. We missed and loved each other. We had an incredibly special relationship that matured as we did.

Then automatically my right hand went out, palm up. "Okay, let's have it," I demanded in a firm voice.

"You mean you don't want me to drive? I'll be happy to drive. How do you think I got here?" My father was smiling as we played this game, he knew I was going to win.

"G-d only knows," I muttered to myself. "Daddy, just give me the keys, please." And of course, he does. This is another of our trip rituals. "Thank you. Now let's put the luggage away and get in the car and get out of this airport."

Fifteen minutes pass when Daddy says, "You know, while you are here, there are a couple of things I'd like you to do for me. I can't do them by myself, so I'd like you to come with me. I want you to enjoy yourselves too, but I have just a few things..." and his voice trails off.

Tony and I rolled our eyes in unison and exchanged knowing 'I told you so' glances as our lips turn up slightly at the ends in almost-smiles.

"You may or may not know this, but I have a little trouble with my hearing," My dad picked up the conversation again, "And I would like you to accompany me to the audiologist where I will be tested and see if I need a hearing aid." Tony and I chimed in articulately and loudly, "Sure, Dad, no problem." Again, we are holding back righteous smiles.

When we were in his apartment, we found the neatly cut-out advertisement for the free appointment. He never tears coupons out like I do. He cuts them with precision. "My goodness, it's for 2 p.m. today, Daddy. I am shocked." To Tony I whispered, "Thank goodness our plane was on time or else we would be tinkering with his schedule."

We ate a quick lunch and were off to the appointment. The audiologist was going to test Daddy to determine the degree of hearing loss. We sat in a small minimally decorated office with the doctor across his polished wood desk. Daddy sat somewhat leaning forward and slumping. Tony and I sat on the periphery behind Daddy to the left and the right in different corners, each of us observing.

At the audiologist's direction, Daddy put a Walkman-like headset on. The doctor was going to send high-pitched tones to one ear at a time from the very complex-looking equipment on his desk that has many faceted meters and panels. The instructions were for Daddy to raise his right hand as soon as he heard something, anything.

I sat about ten feet from my father and heard the tone loud and clear. Daddy, however, is sitting with his back to me, his shoulders hunched over, waiting for something to happen. No hand is ever raised, let alone the right one. Except for this piercing tone, there is absolute silence in the room.

When the other ear was tested, he finally raised his right hand. Yippee, he heard the tone. My ears, however, were still ringing from the overflowing volume of sound.

The results were no surprise. He is profoundly deaf. The audiologist adjusted each side of the headset, like what happens when you have your eyes examined, adjusting it to make up for his deficit. Daddy now had a prescription to each ear, bringing him up to snuff, or as close as you can get to snuff when one is profoundly hearing impaired. The audiologist invited me to whisper to him. From my seat, I softly said in the quietest whisper I can summon, "Daddy, can you hear me?"

Suddenly Daddy sat up, spine straight, shoulders back. His head came up and he turned with raised eyebrows, looking very alert and stunned, and said, "Yes, I can." There was a half-smile of amazement and joy on his face.

All three of us thought this was marvelous. However, here comes the hitch. Daddy asked, "What is the price?" The insurance company doesn't provide these hearing aids, only the kind that goes behind the ear. Daddy doesn't like those. He also doesn't want to pay anything out of his own pocket. He quietly returned to his slumped-shoulder position, looking like one of those blow-up dolls when the air is almost knocked out of their sails in slow motion.

Now, of course, we leave. I stutteringly said, "But, but, Daddy, what a miracle. You could hear me whisper. You sat up so straight. There was such a difference in your ability to hear, wasn't there?"

"Yes, but you know, I can hear. I hear what I want to hear. I play cards often, you know that. I don't need to hear when the other person has gin."

"But, Daddy, aren't you being a little stubborn?" I carefully asked. After all, I didn't want him to be mad at me.

"So what, I have done fine all these years. I'll be fine now."

"But, Daddy, you can't hear! Why let the money stand in the way?"

Tony chimed in at this point with, "Jack, you really ought to reconsider."

Daddy is very obstinate and pretended he doesn't hear either of us now. Once again, Tony and I exchanged glances that said, 'Case closed. Why bother? He's never going to change his mind.'

And he never did.

Have Teeth, Will Travel

My father complained, "My teeth are killing me." Let me be specific and say, he means his full set of dentures! "They're rubbing my gums. It feels like there's a rough spot, and something keeps cutting into me. Oh, you don't know, it's so sore."

"Well," I said with much compassion, "That's too bad, Daddy. Why don't you call your dentist and see if he can see you this afternoon? I'll drive you there."

"I can't go," he wailed. "His office is too far from the elevator. I can't walk that far. No, I can't go," he repeated stubbornly.

I telephoned the dentist and said, "Dr. Johnson, my dad is having difficulties with his dentures. He says they're rubbing and scratching him. What should we do?"

Dr. Johnson immediately responded, "Oh, that's too bad. No problem. Bring him in today at one o'clock this afternoon. Is that OK with him?"

"There is a slight obstacle, doctor. My father can't walk all the way to your office. He says you are too far from the elevator. I was wondering whether there is any other way we can manage this?"

Silence ensued for a minute or so and then I inquired, "Doctor, could I bring his teeth in without him?"

It sounded like he had covered the mouthpiece of the phone with his hand and told those around him – his receptionist, hygienists, and assistant that Mr. Miller was having a problem with his dentures, but he couldn't come in. Any suggestions?

I could barely hear the muffled conversation, but I could clearly hear laughter as they all pondered this challenge.

"You see," Dr. Johnson began, "We need an impression so I can see where and how it's hitting, cutting, or rubbing his gums. Otherwise, I would just be guessing, and we won't take care of the problem."

"How can we do this without my father? Is there something you can suggest?" I asked hopefully.

Again, it sounded like his hand was over the mouthpiece, and I heard the muffled conversation. This time I couldn't make out what's being said. Dr. Johnson and his team suggested a cold cream impression. He explained what that was, and I said OK, I would be there sometime that afternoon.

I reported the conversation to my father and left in search of Pond's Cold Cream, the only name I knew. My targeted mission was successful, and I was back in twenty minutes.

I lined his dentures with this yucky substance, smoothed the top level, and walked towards my father. I spoke very slowly, enunciating each word. "Okay, Dad, let's do this. You put your teeth in perfectly for the first time and bite down on the cold cream. Then I want you to very carefully remove your teeth so that the impression is distinct, and I will take it from there."

As I watched my father, my face went into contortions. It was like when I observed another person brushing their teeth. My mouth went in all directions, my nose crinkled up, and my lips were extended far beyond my teeth. I was truly making distorted circles with my mouth. Perhaps this was involuntary identification. Finally, whatever it was, I had to look away.

There was excess cold cream on his gums, which must have tasted awful, but at the time I did nothing about it.

My job was to be like air cargo people delivering a live, beating heart. I carefully put the teeth in a box, carried it as still as possible in front of me, and zoomed to the dentist. Dr. Johnson's office was about ten minutes away, but I was afraid that the hot, humid heat of Florida would melt the cold cream and it would be an aborted mission.

There were seven traffic lights between Dad's apartment and the office building. I counted them. You guessed it. I got stuck at red at each light.

Finally, I arrived at the building and quickly found a spot just footsteps away. As I walked into the main entrance, there was a sign: "Valet Parking Only. Offenders will be towed away." That was a first for me—valet parking at an office building? Give me a break. Plus, I was only going to be there for a few minutes.

Should I risk being towed away? I remembered Dad telling me how far the office was from the elevator. Was he exaggerating or was it true? Would it take me longer than I expected because of how much walking I had to do? I also had to wait for the doctor to be available and then take care of the teeth. How long would it take to fix the roughness, or even find it fast enough before the cold cream melted? Just thinking about it again had my face doing contortions.

I returned to the car and drove to the front, literally two parking spots away, followed the rules, and had them valet-park the car.

There were three patients in the waiting room; the receptionist and two hygienists were behind the glass partition. I slid open the half window and told them who I was. I heard tittering from the peanut gallery. Our creativity was unique. As a rule, I learned that people didn't have family members dropping off teeth belonging to other family members.

I stared straight ahead, maintaining a poker face, and waited patiently for the dentist to do his deed. When he was done, I once again had the dentures in the box, held carefully in front of me, like a new heart, and I was on my way.

But first I had to proffer my parking stub to the attendant, wait for him to bring the car, tip him for his effort, and be on my merry way back.

Of course, on the return trip, all seven traffic lights were green, and I was back at Dad's side with his teeth ground as smooth as a baby's cheek. He put his teeth in, and we waited with bated breath for the sign that they were OK.

Finally, after several adjustments, since there were remains of cold cream on all surfaces, he said, "Good job, Rosanne!" And that made it all worth it.

Honeydew Melon (My Version)

IT WAS YOUR TYPICAL, tropical-hot, sticky, humid, bright, glary, sun-shining Florida summer day. You've read dad's version; this is mine.

We had our bathing suits on under lightweight, red-checked short-sleeve shirts and what we called our beach shoes. They were white thong-type floppy sandals for me. Dad wore his black, red, and white striped corduroy slip-on bedroom slippers.

We were on a mission. I had recently tasted honeydew melon liqueur and we were searching for it in the liquor stores of Hallandale close to where mom and dad lived. Dad loved honeydew so I was hell-bent to have him taste this wonderful concoction.

The first package store (liquor store language in Florida) had heard of it but responded, "Sorry, not in stock. However, we have something called Creamsicle that is new. Would you like to taste it? We're running a promotion this week."

We were familiar with the name Creamsicle, thanks to the Good Humor Man. We said yes and sipped little sample cups. It was good, but we needed to stay on purpose. We were on a mission.

The second establishment gave us a similar story. The bottom line: no melon liquor. They too were previewing and promoting a new drink. So once again we imbibed this Creamsicle.

By now we were hot and drippy, and the sun was even stronger. Midday had arrived. The humidity had risen, and Dad's patience was wearing thin.

"Enough already. Let's go home. It's not so important anyway," he said in a rather gruff voice.

"One more store, please," I pleaded. "If they don't have it, we'll go home, OK?"

"It's too hot to argue with you. But this is the last store. Let's get going."

As we pulled into the next and last shopping center, a police cruiser was slowly passing. Dad and I exchanged amused glances. After all, here we were in bathing suits with liquor fresh on our breath.

Dad said with a chuckle, "You know, I don't have anything with me. No ID, no driver's license, no credit cards, not even any money."

I chimed in, "I have twenty dollars and the car keys. That's it for me!"

What a combination we were. We laughed again and luckily the cruiser continued cruising.

As we entered the liquor store and walked towards the counter, I once again said, "Please tell us you have heard of Midori and that you have it. You know, it's that honeydew melon liqueur?"

The clerk, much to my amazement, said, "Yes, I have heard of it, and yes, we have it. Please, right this way. And by the way," he said as we were following him up the aisle, "we have a promotion on today for Creamsicle. Would you like to try it?"

Dad and I once again exchanged glances, smiled, and decided one more wouldn't hurt us. But first we got the Midori. While we were paying with my twenty-dollar bill, we sampled yet another Creamsicle.

As soon as we got home, I mixed the Midori with ice in the blender. It was a beautiful shade of light green, the color of ripe honeydew melon. And yes indeed, Dad loved it! Thank goodness. It was all worth it.

My Mom's Passing

MY MOTHER DIED VERY suddenly on March 17, 1989, at the age of 89. She went to the hospital for a pre-arranged ulcer test, and my father accompanied her only because it was raining so he couldn't play golf. She had chest pains while there and so they kept her overnight. My father called to tell me this later in the day. Though he seemed calm, I asked, "Should I come right now?" He said, "No, let's wait to see what the doctor says. You come tomorrow."

I called the hospital and spoke with the night nurse in intensive care and asked her to "Please send my love and my children's love for a speedy recovery to my mom." The nurse told us, "I'll be happy to. To update you, she either had a mild heart attack or is stressed out."

At two a.m., the phone rang. Tony grabbed the phone and my hand at the same time. It was my father. He squeezed my hand so hard I thought he'd break my fingers off. Then the two words we didn't want to hear. "She died. Oh, my G-d, what am I going to do," my father screeched.

I was a lunatic. I had stopped smoking exactly two months prior on January 17th and I was screaming and crying at the same time, walking around like Groucho Marx, "I want a cigarette, I want a cigarette." No one paid any attention to me, and there were no cigarettes in the house.

At that time, Eastern Airlines was flying from New York to Florida. It was Friday and Spring break, and the airlines were overbooked. Truth be told, my mother would have killed me or at the least haunted me if I didn't come. My father was catatonic on the phone. He kept repeating, "What am I going to do. What am I going to do…" He was walking around in circles.

My family in New York did get tickets and off we went. My father picked us up at the airport wearing dark-green slacks and a light-green button-down shirt. He had laid his clothes out the night before and now it's the seventeenth of March—St. Patrick's Day.

From the airport we went directly to the funeral home to make final arrangements. My father was a wreck, looked like he'd aged twenty-five years. I was in take-charge mode and would do my crying later.

But I wanted to see my mother. That isn't allowed I was told. "I don't care what your rules are. I want to see my mother," I said with my voice four octaves higher. Then I stared the guy in the eye and said nothing. He brought my mother out for all of us to see her. "That's not my mother," I kept repeating. Tony said, "Ro, it's your mother." "No, it's not. She never wore makeup." They had makeup on her. I finally calmed down and we left. The next morning, we dropped off the sky-blue silk short-sleeve dress she wore to our wedding and her bedroom slippers, which she preferred to wear. I thought she'd get a kick out of that.

I had these two thoughts, 'If she saw me with my new permed hair, she'd love me.' And then immediately, 'Whew, what a relief. I can stop trying to get her to love me.'

My father was in bad shape—I thought I would lose him too. I did my best to be there for him, but I lost it at one point and yelled at him, "You know you're not the only one in pain! I lost my mother!" That may have been the first time I ever raised my voice to my father.

My father was a religious man, but never would he say he was a spiritual being. From where I sit, our relationship, not all the time, but sometimes, was beyond the realm of understanding. It didn't fit into a cubby, and it wasn't limited by the box we live in. It has its place in what I call DI, Divine Intervention.

Had I not written these stories, no, if I had not written them thirty plus years ago and lost and then found them in a file folder stuck between two three-ring notebooks with the plastic pockets in front standing on a shelf in my office as we were packing on moving day, none of this would be within my reach.

It's like seeing him/me/her through a different lens, one that has no boundaries, no rules, no barriers. It just is and flows and grows, soft like cotton and hard like steel.

Dad & Joe and Ann & Me

AFTER MY MOM PASSED, my father came to visit us in our home in Connecticut. The back of his hand was still sore from an intravenous needle from some minor surgery. Melody, our dog, was a decent size, half German Shepherd and half Doberman, maybe fifty pounds and a very important member of our family. We had her since she was a puppy, and she was great with people. She sensed his hand hurt and would gently put her head under the palm of that hand and slowly raise it to get him to pay her attention, being ever so careful, as if she sensed its tenderness, and she was right. They both reacted sweetly to one another, my father was caught off guard and touched and my sensitive dog seemed to smile. Whatever guests were privy to this were misty-eyed as they also were moved by what you'd call a 'Kodak moment,' or in today's world, a photo op. They had a special relationship and language known only to them. The eyes showed the love that existed between them.

Our guests were milling around the wafting barbeque smells of ribs, chicken, steak, and the pool. We decided to invite all our friends (mostly in their fifties like me at the time) to meet my father. He was happy for the honor and the opportunity to meet some of the people he had only heard about. Dad loved talking to people and they sure enjoyed his stories, rapt in their attention. It was as if he were holding court, getting energized by the attention and the storytelling and, of course, the intent listening of his euphoric audience. This time he turned to Melody, and asked, "Which story should I tell?" Melody cocked her head left and right as if pondering her recommendation.

Dad said, "Ok, I got it. Thanks, Mel."

"The Honeydew liqueur story. Rosanne and I were coming home from the beach, both in beachwear, and we stopped at the liquor store. Rosanne wanted to introduce me to this honeydew liqueur since she knows how much I love the melon."

What's so special about this story? We tasted some other sample liqueurs and purchased a bottle and walked to the car. "Dad, do you have your license with you?" "Nope, do you?" he asked. My answer was, "Nope." "And you used up all your money, right?" "Yep," I continued, "And you don't have your driver's license, no form of ID, and we both smell of liquor? We must be extra careful. Perhaps you should let me drive! Keys please." And he told this story slowly very similar to my version and as if he were reliving every moment. Everyone shared a good chuckle from this story which united us over the hilarity of the situation. We did make it back home without incident.

He always reminds me of those large blow-up characters that, as they're being filled with helium, they slowly unfold from the knees to the waist to the chest and then straight up. That was my father. Our friends hung onto his every word, and I'm sure it motivated them to reach out to their own parents when they got home.

My father came alive when there was someone to talk to. He had color in his face, his hazel-green eyes were sparkling, and his hands were constantly in the air emphasizing a point or just animated.

At one point, Joe, my good friend Ann's father, sat next to my father by the pool. Joe looked over at my father. "You know, I lost my wife recently," he said softly and slowly. My father responded, "Oh no, sorry. Me, too. When did your wife pass, was it recent?" "Yes, March 17th, Yours?" "March 17th." There was a pause and then: "What?"

"Yes, the same day, this is beyond coincidence." We captured it in a photo to remember this moment.

As they continued to exchange information, they learned what we had known all along, that our mothers—Ann's and mine—died on the same day. When the 'fathers' found this out they were taken aback, their expressions a mix of astonishment and wonder. Instantly there was a bond between them. The surprise on their faces was priceless. The immediate connection was palpable. We were as moved as they were, even though we knew about it!

During the rest of the party and for days after, Dad was still talking about Joe and how much they had in common, and he said, "Can you imagine? Wasn't that something? They died on the same day." Often, he talked to Melody about my mother and also Joe. He asked Melody, "Do you remember Grandma, Melody?" Her eyes glued on my father's as if to say, "Of course I do."

When I called Ann to tell her my mother had passed, her husband answered the phone with, "How did you know so soon? Who told you?"

I was stunned. "What are you talking about?" He thought I knew Ann's mom had passed but I was calling to say my mom had passed. Two best friends lost their mothers on the same day. It still stops me in my tracks. My hope is that they are friends in Heaven as we daughters are in this world.

We, of course, took many pictures of them together. Ann told me Joe kept his copy in his room where he could see it every day. He was a very sweet man and very touched by the conversations with my dad. The sharing of their loss was visceral.

Last Trip to Connecticut

THAT WAS HIS LAST trip to visit us. As he often said, "It's easier if you come to me in Florida. I am more comfortable in my own home now." We did know this to be true.

We had a lovely house with a wraparound deck with entry from the dining room, family room, or living room. Woods were behind us and on our sides, so it was a very peaceful, serene, quiet environment.

Dad didn't see the step off the dining room to the deck and fell. I learned what it felt like to have your heart in your throat. I heard him call me and I ran and got him up. At that point, I wanted to put him on a leash. I had told him, "Wait for me and we'll go outside together and sit for a while and let the sun warm our bones." But no, he wanted to do it when he wanted to do it. At ninety-plus he was still as stubborn as ever. Luckily, he wasn't badly hurt, and he was micro-supervised from then on.

He was right, though. He was more comfortable in his own surroundings. It was our honor to visit him and he, of course, loved it. He would sit on his terrace with Tony and the two would chat away until they both put each other to sleep. It was a sight to see. Another 'photo op' as we created more memories which always leave us with a smile.

It's a warm feeling to remember these tender moments. They help to neutralize and balance the not-so-tender moments. I have tools to cope today whereas my father's generation had none. He was the man in the family and that came with responsibility, not touchy-feely things. Only when he was older did he soften and share his feelings as well as his thoughts.

PERSONAL PLEA!

Thank You for Reading My Book!

I really appreciate all your feedback and
I love hearing what you have to say.
I need your input to make the next version of this book and any future
books better.

Please take two minutes now to leave a helpful review on Amazon letting
me know what you thought of the book

Thanks so much!
Rosanne D'Ausilio, PhD, Author

Moving Day

IT'S A BRAND-NEW APARTMENT for my dad, his first move in thirty years. He picked it out himself. A widower of almost two years at the time, he had been living in the condo that he and my mom shared for those thirty years, ever since they moved to Florida from Ohio. I'm sure my mom had been most influential wherever they lived, how they decorated, what went in which closets, and on which shelves were the shirts or the sweaters.

This very large one-bedroom, two-bath apartment was in a high-rise building across the street from the ocean and around the corner from the previous condo. He subleased it from the owner on a yearly basis. This property had tennis courts, handball courts, a pool, a Jacuzzi, a card room, a pool room, and many more active people than where he previously lived.

Even though he chose the apartment himself, he called me. "Rosanne, I want you to come to Florida and help me move. I'll get everything packed, you help me move and unpack. When can you come?" I heard, by the tone of his voice that he wanted me there yesterday. How to refuse? Of course, I came. He even sweetened the pot by paying my airfare. I was flying from our home in Connecticut to Ft. Lauderdale.

Because the two apartments—old and new—were about five minutes apart, we moved the cartons by car. My dad had already unloaded a number of them, so we had only a few trips remaining when I arrived.

What he specifically wanted me to do was to unpack and put things where they should go. For instance, he didn't know which should be the linen closet, or on what shelf to put the dishes and glasses in the kitchen. This was something my mother always did.

He was, however, noticeably clear about his bedroom walk-in closet. Slacks and shorts on one side, shirts hanging in color order on another. Nothing could go above the first shelf. Why? Because he couldn't reach any higher and I certainly didn't want him standing on a chair or a step stool. (He was ninety-one at this time.)

Luggage could go on the second shelf, though. That's where I put it, but that wasn't good enough. He didn't like opening the closet and looking at suitcases. He said, "Leave it, I don't want it there. I can see it first thing. Leave it, I'll move it later!" I had visions of him standing on a chair to move the suitcase and losing his balance, falling, breaking a hip, etc. I hopped on a chair and kept moving the suitcase until he was happy. At one point I had the thought of hitting him on the head with it, I must admit. The goal was that it could not be seen from the room or even when you first walked into the closet.

Eleven large cartons later, I was beat and needed to rest. I wanted to go to the pool and sit in the sun. He wanted to keep going. I didn't want him to get mad at me, so I continued doing whatever he asked. I was very aware there were no buffers there, no one to protect me if he got mad at me. I was noticing my reaction, and then... Two cartons later, he suggested, "Let's take a break and go to the pool." I almost fell over. We did go and he said, "This is nice, isn't it?" After an hour or two we were back at work.

The next day we went to the pool again and met very nice people. I taught him how to climb up the steps at the deep end of the pool and introduced him to the Jacuzzi, which he loved. He looked so happy to have people around to chat with about nothing, something, or nonsense. Of course, these were younger people because people his own age weren't fun for him. "They're old," he would say.

His apartment's master bathroom had a Roman bathtub. To the day he died, I was the only one who ever used it. Dad only took showers. Had my mother lived, I think she'd have loved the apartment. Even though she never wanted to live in a high-rise building, it was actually quite nice.

Over lunch he kept asking me if I was happy. "Are you happy? Are you really happy? Are you sure?" I replied, "I'm happier than I've ever been. Yes, I am."

He was also preparing for his demise. He would say, "You know, I'm starting to get old. I feel surprisingly good, but let's face it. I'm not getting any younger. It could happen tomorrow, a week, a month, a year from now. I want to be sure you and your sister are taken care of." My eyes would well up with tears and I got real quiet and just listened. I think he knew how much I loved and needed him. Maybe that's why he stayed around so long. His favorite analogy was to say, "My body is like a car, eventually the parts wear out."

He was very proud of his new place and took great care of it. He drove to the stores, shopped, cooked, cleaned, and did everything for himself. He also lied about his age to get into this building. He told people he was in his early eighties when in fact he was in his early nineties.

Although on the same floor as his apartment, the laundry room was a far walk for him. So what did he do? He attached a rope to his laundry basket and pulled it to and from the room. Why? Because it was too heavy for him to carry. It looked like he had a pet on a leash.

His parking space under the building was also far away. A friend of his in the building lost his license and sold his car. My father was able to get to his space, which was much closer to the entry to the building. Yes, he drove at ninety-one. However, for the past ten years, when I got off the plane my hand went out. "Keys, please."

"Oh, you don't want me to drive?" my father asked.

My response was, "Keys, please, or I'm back on that plane!"

He ultimately lost his license because he couldn't pass the eye exam. This is so my father. He had a cataract operation, healed, was re-tested and got his license back. I can't believe the Motor Vehicle Bureau did so, but he passed the eye test.

However, he knew his reflexes weren't really swift, so he went out early in the morning to run errands when there was less traffic. He went to the store, the bank, and the bakery, usually in that order. He never drove at night or when it was beginning to get dark out.

Being able to drive and take care of himself allowed him to keep his dignity and independence. He was certainly a role model for me as to what's possible, regardless of age.

My father lived to ninety-four, my mother to eighty-nine, and to this day I don't know what 'old' is and as I write this, I'm eighty-two. My grandparents were all gone before I was born so my parents were my role models. Bless them for giving me a gift they had no idea they gave me.

Midsummer Night's Dream

IT WAS A HOT, muggy, shirt-stick-to-your-back kind of day in June.
As I disembarked the plane in Southern Florida. I realized this
was the first time in almost thirty years I had visited my father
alone... no buffers. No husband, children, mother, or sister was
present. My heart skipped a beat as I wondered whether this was
significant. Patience and time would tell. My thoughts kept getting
my attention. 'What if he gets mad at me, what will I do? Who will
help me?' I was back to walking on eggs. 'Wait, I'm not a child. It'll
be fine.' And on it went. My self-talk worked, and I was back in the
present.

My job, being Superwoman in the family, was to, within one
week's time, arrange for round-the-clock help so my father would be
well taken care of, negotiate the best possible financial arrangement,
get his house in order, do his banking, shopping, cooking, washing...
and whatever else he wanted to add to that.

I was scared to really 'see' him. And rightly so. He looked twenty
years older than my visit six months before. He'd lost weight, his face
was sallow, his false teeth were on the table next to him rather than
in his mouth. He was sitting upright on a chair, looking sad and lost,
covered by an afghan I had crocheted for him.

When he saw me, we cried together and held hands staring into each other's eyes. He repeated over and over, "I'm so glad you're here. I am so happy to see you. I missed you so much I couldn't wait for today to come when you would be here." Then I went into action. We each had our lists and we kept adding to them.

Why is this sudden attention needed on my part? My father went to his bank which had shiny black marble see-your-face-in-it floors with a step up into the lobby. There was, and still is, nothing to show there's a step, or a sign that says "Watch Your Step" or be careful. We are in Florida with senior people, after all.

He didn't see the step—truth be told, I didn't see it either until the last second. But my reflexes were better than his, as was my eyesight.

He tripped up the step, fell, and got himself up because he was on a mission, after all, to do his banking. He took care of his transactions and proceeded to leave and yes, you guessed it. This time he fell face-down on his way out. And this time he hurt himself and the bank put him in a taxi, and it took him home.

His Call for Help

HE REALLY HURT HIMSELF and had problems getting up from a chair, a couch, and also the toilet. He was heard moaning and calling for help one day. When the administration of the building found him, they told him he'd have to move. The alternative was they would put him in a 'home.'

That's when I got the call. "Can you come down here and help me? I seem to have fallen and if you don't help me, the building will put me in a home." That's all I needed to hear. Rosie to the rescue. I booked a flight and was there as soon as I could. My sister picked me up at the airport and drove me to my father's apartment. She told me, "You had best prepare yourself. He doesn't look good." She scared me, but at least I was warned.

Please note that my sister, sixteen years my senior, lived twenty-five to thirty minutes away. But she wouldn't do. I was who he wanted to help him, not her.

I was brought up to respect my parents, and it was instilled in me it was my job to take care of them if/when they couldn't take care of themselves. And I was and am a woman of my word. This theory was never put to the test with my mother because she was very active. She was an avid golfer and bowler and played golf two days prior to her death. So, she got her wish, to go like a lady and quickly, which she did, leaving us all shell-shocked in the process.

Although my father was ninety-three at the time, in my mind's eye he was in his seventies. He was very active, vibrant, played golf regularly, lived alone, cooked, and did his own laundry. He drove a car... not when I was around, but he did drive. You could easily see him coming from afar. His was the car that looked like there was no driver behind the steering wheel. He looked through it rather than over it. But that was before his accident.

My Dad's apartment had a pull-out couch in the living room. This particular pull-out had metal all the way around it. How do I know that? Because each time I got out of it, I got a new set of bruises on my legs.

By the end of the first day, before I was even totally unpacked, we had attacked his list and had help in place for him and a negotiated fee for three caregivers. We didn't need nurses, just someone to be at his beck and call for meals, showers, and tidying up (that part didn't get handled very well, I'm sorry to say). It got added to the list.

For the week I was there, I was on the night shift. Each night he was up every two or three hours. Once for water, one time for the bathroom, one time to see if it was morning yet.

After the first night, I learned to sleep through the moans and groans and only respond to my name. I would go to sleep when he did, 8–9 p.m. Thus, I got three to four unbroken hours of sleep before the ritual began.

After three nights of interrupted sleep and having been up with him twice already this one night, my patience was worn thin. However, this time he seemed really agitated and upset, saying repeatedly, "I'm not making it up. I really mean it. It's true. I'm not making it up." I came to him and asked, "Who are you talking to?" as it clearly wasn't me. He said, "My daddy. He's in the other room."

With no teeth in his mouth and weighing perhaps 110 pounds, he looked at that moment like a young boy of maybe 12. I kept asking him where his father was. He kept saying, "He's in there. He's in the other room. He's going to be so angry." Then I remembered his father's picture was hanging in the dining room.

I said very seriously, "I saw your daddy in the dining room, too." He looked up with quite an amazed expression on his face. His mouth dropped open, his eyebrows raised, and he said, "You did?"

"Yes, I did, and he told me to tell you to go to sleep right now!" Well, it worked. He laid his little head down without a peep and went right to sleep.

In the morning, no mention was made of his dream. But he did tell me how sorry he was to have woken me so many times. I thought this was quite unusual. I've never forgotten it. Interesting the little gems we take with us into our future.

Last Days with Dad

IN HIS LAST DAYS, he was constantly reviewing his financial status, his assets, his investments, the balance in his checking account, and wouldn't buy or spend beyond what was necessary. Growing up he never had a credit card, didn't believe in them. His position was that by the time you got the bill, you had already used whatever it was you bought. That applied to his cars as well. He drove a Cadillac and paid cash for it and traded it every two years, with very little cash changing hands.

Our Daily Routine

One morning I was up automatically at 5 a.m. After all, if for four mornings in a row your dad woke up at 5 a.m. and then woke you up, by the fifth day you, too, would be on this routine, no? However, I am now the only one up, except of course for the birds and the sun. The silence is broken by birdsong and the thrown shadows as the sun slowly rises to the start of a new day.

I stand by and watch my father sleep. My irrational mind is looking for movement, more precisely, breathing. Where is the gentle rise and fall of the chest in peaceful repose? I stare at the blanket, but it doesn't seem to move. Now I'm getting scared. Is he dead? Did he die in his sleep? What a wonderful way to go. Why doesn't he move? I sense it's my paranoia. He's only sleeping, isn't he? I check on him every ten minutes. So far so good.

While he sleeps, I can really look at him. So this is what he looks like, I say to myself. Wow, he sure is a small man, half his stature. He sleeps on his side like a child. Head on the pillow, hands under the pillow held together as if praying. His face is relaxed but worn-out looking. For one instance I think, 'I don't know this person in bed. This is not my father who was always meticulous about himself. This man has a growth on his face, no teeth in his mouth, and unruly hair.'

An hour passed, and he finally awakens. With his eyes open and alert, my daddy is back. We made it to another day. If I keep up this vigilance, I'm not going to outlive him!

Bathroom toiletries are next. With my help, he's up and using the walker, shuffling off to the bathroom. His routine begins. Toilet, wash hands, wet face with a hot washcloth. Shave with an electric razor, stare aimlessly. Put teeth in the mouth. Then put the comb in your left hand. Raise left arm by placing the right hand under the elbow, palm up, and pushing up to comb his hair. You see, he fell up concrete steps, lost his balance, and fell right into the step, and severely hurt his arm. With my help he gets dressed, though he chooses his own outfit for the day. He still asserts his independence whenever he can.

Breakfast & the Shuffle

NOW WE'RE GOING INTO the kitchen for breakfast. You can't prepare ahead for this man as he has very specific ideas as to what he wants and when. Today's choice is one half a grapefruit, sectioned please, with one Sweet n' Low sprinkled on top, and dry toast, one slice, not too dark. Simple enough.

After breakfast, he shuffles to a chair in the living room closest to the sliding glass doors so he can catch the sunrise. This is where he holds court daily until bedtime. His pillows get fluffed, the afghan gets tucked around him, and his day is now ahead of him. With the telephone to his right and his address book tucked under his left leg, he can make and receive phone calls. We also have two glasses by the phone. One with 7Up so he will stay hydrated (he hates water), and the other is for urinating easily without having to get up and shuffle to the bathroom.

Now that he is comfortably positioned, my chores for the day begin. I make the bed, get today's newspaper, and take out the garbage. For some reason, garbage can't stay in his apartment for more than one hour. It must go out.

We have the same daily conversation now. Money. What is coming in from the CDs, stock, and social security? What is going out in rent, telephone, gas, and food? And then what is the difference, and what do

I think? Is he OK? We add the numbers over and over. We even get a calculator and add the numbers again. They keep coming out the same.

It's at this point I ask myself, 'Who is the parent and who is the child here?' Our roles feel reversed to me. I give him reassurance that all is well. The numbers game is over for this day.

Before I turn around, it's lunchtime. He eats next to nothing. His favorite is a grilled cheese sandwich made by frying it in butter with the cover on to steam the cheese and golden-brown the bread. He likes it cut into bite-size pieces with a few slices of fresh, ripe, red tomato. After taking four small morsels, he's done. "Please don't make me eat anymore. I just can't." So, I don't.

Neighbors drop in or call almost daily. Harry, who recently lost his wife, lives on another floor in his building. Before her death Dad used to drive Harry to the hospital to visit her. He tells Harry, "I'm getting better. We'll go driving again soon." Harry believes this. I believe him too. After all, he is a very determined man who usually gets his way. His attitude is positive, and he is quite sure he is on the mend.

After a month of no notable change in his overall health, i.e., he can't get up from the chair alone, he gestures for me to come closer. He does this by crooking his pointer finger in a 'come here' motion His crooking means, 'Come here, no come a little closer!' And he said, "Rosanne, do you think I'll ever get better?" My decisive moment. Do I tell him what he wants to hear or my opinion? Do I have one? Are they one and the same?

Taking a deep breath, "Well, Daddy, I don't know. But I don't think you'll be able to drive again."

He looked at me out of the corner of his eye. He didn't like my answer. He was quite an independent man just a few weeks ago. He lived alone, shopped by himself, drove himself where he had to go, cooked, cleaned, and did a good job of it all. He sat in quiet thought and dozed for about an hour.

Just before bedtime, he said, "If I don't get better, I don't want to be here." That really scared me. I know how important attitude is, and if he gives up, well, I wasn't ready for that. I was up all night checking to be sure he was breathing.

The next morning, he was bright and cheerful. I had been up all night worried it was his last. I said, "Oh, you changed your mind?" somewhat sarcastically. He chose not to answer me.

Hospice

I WAS ON THE phone with my father's doctor asking what our options were for him. The doctor said, "We can put him in hospice. It's a wonderful organization and service." I was confused and said, "He doesn't have cancer." I then was educated on what hospice was. "He has six months or less to live." "Wow, OK, what do we do?" He told us there would be nurses coming in to take his vitals and to interview him.

The next day, just as the doctor said, someone came to interview him. We thought he'd have to qualify and so he put on an act of moaning. He qualified without moaning.

Every day a nurse came, and we felt so supported and cared for.

Rabbi Bob

"DAD, HOW ABOUT IT, would you like to have a rabbi come and visit you tonight?"

"Could I? Would one come?" he asked with amazement. Hospice offers this service, something neither one of us knew.

"I think so. It says in this service-oriented pamphlet that religious visits are available. I'll call and see." I made the call and shared the results with my father.

"Here's the deal, Dad. They can't promise, but they'll try. It's 4 p.m. on a Friday and Friday nights are busy nights for rabbis, what with Sabbath Services. However, they've assured me they will see what they can do."

From the few days' experience we have now had with Hospice, their routine is normally they call and say someone will be here at such and such a time and their name is so-and-so. When no one contacted us by 7 p.m., we both figured it wasn't going to happen. Oh well, we'd given it the old college try.

At 7:20 p.m. the front desk attendant of his apartment building called to say someone was on their way up. I opened the door in anticipation, not knowing who or what to expect. A young man was walking towards me, casually dressed. In Florida terms, which means no tie or sports jacket. He was tall, maybe just under six feet, very light skinned, and had short reddish-brown hair. I asked in a loud whisper "Are you the clergyman from Hospice?"

He said, "Yes," and nodded his head at the same time. He continued walking towards me. "Are you a rabbi?" I asked hopefully.

"No," he shyly replied. "Sorry, I am not."

"Would you be willing to be a rabbi for us just for tonight?" I couldn't believe I was asking him this outrageous question.

To my utter amazement, he said, "Sure. I just hope no one asks me to read or pray in Hebrew." I found myself chuckling and smiling. We had someone with a sense of humor. My father would love it.

"What is your name?" I expected to hear 'Father So-and-So and held my breath as he answered, "Bob."

By now we were entering the apartment together. We slowly approached my father, and I said, "Daddy, this is Rabbi Bob. He came to see you. Isn't that great?"

My father looked both astounded and pleased at the same time as he said, "Pull up a chair real close to me, Rabbi Bob. Sit over here. I'm so happy to see you. I'm so happy you came to visit me. I can't tell you what this means to me." My Dad's hazel-green eyes overflowed with heartfelt tears, and his hands reached out to touch Rabbi Bob.

As Rabbi Bob sat, my father started to question him. "Did you know Rabbi Silver? That's who married me and my wife a long time ago. That was in Cleveland, Ohio. Did you know him?"

Rabbi Bob honestly replied, "No, I'm sorry, can't say that I did. I live in Florida, you see."

"You need to speak up for me, Rabbi Bob, because I don't hear so good anymore. I'm getting older now, you know." My father was ninety-four with all his faculties, except he doesn't hear well, but you read the story about his hearing test.

"You know, Rabbi Bob, I used to sing in the choir when I was a boy." (I never knew this!) Rabbi Bob interjected, "Why don't you sing something for us right now?" Without needing any encouragement, Daddy belts out the Shama Yisroel, a melodious Hebrew song that is sung on the eve of the Sabbath, Friday night, to honor G-d.

My son, Kevin, a grown man at twenty-five, and I were sitting on the couch observing. We were reveling in this divine intervention taking place right before our eyes. One minute we were laughing as if our sides would come off; the next we were moved to tears and were hysterical crying and drenching the couch.

Rabbi Bob and my father continued to sit together quietly, holding hands for a short time, and my father was so calm, content, and happy, he dozed off. I woke him with: "Daddy, is there anything else you want to ask Rabbi Bob? He can't stay here long, you know. He has other places to go, other people to see."

Rabbi Bob interrupted, "Oh, don't worry about me. I'm fine with time. I'm enjoying being here." He turned to my father and said, "Would you like me to pray with you?"

In unison, we all said yes, smiling and feeling so blessed with this possibility. Rabbi Bob prayed for my father individually and then for all of us as a family. Kevin and I had white knuckles from holding hands so tightly for this entire time. I was so touched and moved. I was speechless, with happy/sad tears rolling down my face. Kevin sobbed uncontrollably alongside me.

After the 23rd Psalm was recited, Rabbi Bob took his leave and we all, of course, thanked him profusely. I walked him slowly to the door and, out of earshot of my father, inquired, "So what are you, or how do I even ask this question?"

"I'm a priest. But it was a delight being with your family and especially your incredible father tonight."

As I renter the room, Daddy was saying to Kevin, "He's such a nice young man. I can't believe he took time to come and see me, pray with me, pray for me. Wasn't that something? That was wonderful. Wasn't he such a nice man?" Of course, we all agreed.

About an hour later, my father said, totally out of the blue and unexpected, "Rosanne, I don't know what I did to have such a caring, wonderful daughter, but I love you so much and I'm so proud of you." I think I've waited my whole life to hear these words.

The White Light

JUST BEFORE HIS DEATH, Daddy said, "You know, Dolly," (his favorite name for me), "I really don't want to live like this. If I am never going to get any better than this, I don't want to be here. I am ready to go. Please help me. Don't make me go to any more doctors. Don't make me eat when I'm not hungry. Please."

I responded with, "I will help you, but I won't do anything illegal. I don't want to see you suffer either. I will call Hospice and see what they suggest. But then after you're gone, I want you to watch over me. Will you do that?" He said, "Yes," and my daddy always kept his word.

However, neither of us had the forethought to arrange a code so that I would know he was really watching over me. Like a special phrase, or a color, or a number, or a certain license plate or a particular bird or even a messenger.

***

The next day, July 25th in the year 1992, a warm, sunny, Saturday about 1:30 p.m., my ninety-four--year-old father died peacefully. But I'm getting ahead of myself.

That morning, the Hospice person who came to take his vitals said to me, "He's only hanging on for you. It's time you let go of him." Well,

I was indignant inside, feeling insulted. I thought I had released him. I said, "OK then, put him in the Hospice unit." And I walked away. Kevin meanwhile was sitting with my father holding his hand. My father kept taking off his pinky ring, putting it on Kevin's pinky, and taking it off Kevin and putting it back on his own pinky. Tears were rolling down Kevin's face. It was a special moment and memory for just the two of them. So, I left the room.

The Hospice nurse asked me if I could go to the funeral home and make arrangements. I said, "No, I can't!" Then I added, "But I could call them and say, 'Do for my father as you did for my mother.' And I did. My father would have been so pleased. It was around 10 a.m. When you pre-arrange a funeral, there is a discount for doing so in advance. My father died that afternoon and because of my calling ahead, we saved $500. I can almost feel him smiling as I write this.

When the ambulance came to get him, I stayed as detached as a person could under these circumstances. Again, this Hospice protocol was new to us, including the support from such caring people.

Kevin and I followed him to the hospital in the car. The hospital had one floor which was for Hospice. As we got off the elevator, the ambulance driver saw us and pointed to my father's nurse.

This nurse asked quietly, "Are you the family of Jack Miller?" I nodded, already scared of what he was about to tell us. He said, "Your father was here five minutes and then let go." Zombiesque, Kevin and I went to his room to say our last goodbyes. As we were slowly approaching the room, Kevin turned to me and said, "Mommy"—he hadn't called me 'Mommy' for years—"Mommy, you were right, you were so right to put him in Hospice."

I asked Kevin to call and tell my sister. We had quite different relationships with my father, and I was too exhausted to deal with her.

Because we were there to help my father, we only had swim and tennis wear with us. Into the car we went to Burdine's, a local department store, for appropriate funeral attire. I put the clothes we bought and the funeral on my credit card.

A Real Rabbi

AFTER HIS DEATH, A real rabbi called to compile personal information about my father for the eulogy. I related this emotional story of the night before and 'Rabbi Bob.'

We were then informed, surprised, and our hearts were wrenched wide open for what we learned. This rabbi recited Jewish folklore about how rabbinical students were instructed to make confession the night before they died and how important this was for a Jew and especially for a rabbi.

Naturally one student asked what I wondered too, "But, Rabbi, how do you know when you're going to die so that you will know the night before you die?"

"Good question, the truth is you don't know." The rabbi continued, "That is why you make confession every night."

My father unknowingly made confession, having met with Rabbi Bob the night before he died. That Saturday morning, I never had the opportunity to tell him who Rabbi Bob was because we were so busy with Hospice. My father died with the knowledge he'd made peace with his maker the night before he died. This was and is divine intervention at its highest level for my family and especially for my father.

At his funeral, the real rabbi officiating related this story. Kevin and I were right back to Friday night on the couch crying silently with tears rolling down our faces.

G-d bless you, Daddy—and He did—and we love you to the moon and back. We are blessed with this sacred, precious memory that we share individually and together.

W-H-I-T-E L-I-G-H-T

A MONTH OR SO after his death while I was in the bathtub with the water steaming and the bubbles effervescing, I took a couple of deep breaths and I asked G-d, "Please send me a sign that my father is really watching over me and that he is OK wherever he is. I don't feel his presence and I want to know for sure. Please, G-d."

Soon thereafter I had the vividest (if there is such a word) dream. My husband and I were arriving home from somewhere and I had to go to the bathroom really bad. He pulled into our attached garage. I nearly bolted out of the still-moving car, ran up the steps in the garage, unlocked the door, and continued to speed to the bathroom. I passed the one on the first floor, heading for the second floor's master bath.

The next thing I remember is I am standing facing the mirror over the sink. I looked up and I saw my father in the mirror off to my left. He's dressed in beige khaki pants, a white-on-white short-sleeve shirt with his initials JAM embroidered in dark blue on one pocket, rubber-soled shoes, and blue-and-white checked socks. He is standing on his own volition and smiling at me. Off to the side is another person, perhaps an aide. It reminds me of a photograph where my father is up close and in perfect focus, and the aide or whoever is a blur in the background.

On the vanity counter off to my left is a hurricane lamp in the off position. My father is facing the mirror, same as I am, and we are communicating via our reflections. I'm afraid to turn away or around because it might break whatever was going on here. He said, "Rosanne, it's too dark in here. Make the light, make the white light," with his hand gesturing for me to proceed. I turned on the light as he asked.

Just then another movement caught my eye in the mirror, and, as I looked up, I saw my mother coming towards me, with someone just out of focus, not too far from her also—perhaps another aide. Her walk was solid, and she was dressed in pink Bermuda shorts with a white V-neck tee-shirt and pink half socks and sneakers. Again, I thought there might be communication via the mirror. And then... the phone rang and woke me up.

I truly believe this dream was in answer to my prayers to receive a sign that my father is watching over me. When he was in his last hour on Earth, I was there, talking to him. His eyes were closed, his legs were flailing as though he was walking, and his arms were moving up and down. I said, "Daddy, go towards the light. Walk towards the white light. See if you recognize anyone. Mommy is there and your mommy and daddy too. Walk towards the light. When you get close enough, they will put their arms out to help you cross over." Kevin was privy to this conversation and was rolling his eyes.

About two minutes later he said something I couldn't make out. Instead of asking my usual, "What hurts you, Daddy?" which I had been doing for a week, I said, "What do you see?"

He said in a large whisper, "W-H-I-T-E L-I-G-H-T" drawing out each letter as if it were taffy being pulled from his throat. I was speechless.

For me, this dream reinforces my prayers and belief that my father is watching over me. I do believe it was another what I call DI—Divine Intervention. The more time that has passed since that night, the deeper is my belief that a divine force is taking better care of me than I do.

The Scarf

An incredibly special green silk scarf with red polka dots and soft fringe about three feet long was draped around my neck, fluttering down to around my shoulders as I walked. The softness against my skin evoked memories of a child being fondly caressed by a parent. So long as I wore the scarf, no harm could come to me.

It was so wide it could be doubled and still more than cover the width of my neck. The length was perfect as it crossed itself and fit into the lapels of my camel's-hair full-length Winter coat. It would withstand any sub-zero temperature.

It was worn so thin that the seams were giving way, shredding apart. But the warmth was still there. In truth at first it felt cool to me, but within seconds the warmth emanated throughout my body.

I remembered with love and tenderness the occasions my father had worn this scarf. Up North in Ohio, it was a daily vision. But in the South, only on cool days and often accompanied by a green velvet beret worn cocked to one side, the left, as he complained of the cold.

I loved to fondle the scarf, run it between my fingers, bring it to my face, bury my nose in it, breathe deeply, sniffing the smell of what used to be. It represented roots, love, gentle caring, and brought back vivid memories.

I remember the day my father gave it to me. "Are you sure?" I inquired with raised eyebrows. "After all, when a cold front comes, what are you going to do? You always used to wear it." "No, I want you to have it," he replied, stroking my cheek with his right hand. "I know how much you like it, and it gives me pleasure to know you will wear it up North where it gets really, really cold."

Each time I wrap it around my neck, it is as if my father is holding me, sheltering me from the cold. The satisfied smile on his face when he gave it to me got triggered each time I wore it. It is a wonderful memory I can bring forth at will, just by having the scarf in close proximity.

Sometimes I wear it indoors, just to feel protected and encompassed. The smoothness of the silk calms me on stressful days. It doesn't have to be around my neck—it could be in my lap, in my hands, around my arms, even draped over the back of a chair. I sometimes talk to it because this scarf, as you must have guessed by now, is really my father., I certainly have memories that I wish I didn't. And yet I was cared for and am alive today to tell my story.

Without realizing it until now, my new winter coat is a full-length dark green cloth coat. I have the perfect scarf for it, don't you agree?

Red Cardinals

WHAT'S INCREDIBLY SIGNIFICANT FOR me today is the connection I have with my father. When I have thoughts about him, when I'm writing about him, when it's Father's Day or his birthday, I will look out the window and before my eyes appears a red (male) cardinal. The cardinal stays on the ledge to make sure I see it and acknowledge it and then flies away. A couple of times I feel my father's presence in my house, with his hand on my right shoulder ever so gently. So long as I don't turn around, the image and experience stay with me for a bit. If I do turn around, it's gone. The first time it happened I was afraid he was coming to take me back with him. But that's not the case. And whether it's true or coincidence, my interpretation brings me peace and a visit now and again from my father who has been gone for at least thirty years.

He's watching over me. It always warms my heart, makes me smile and feel peaceful when I see a cardinal. I always say, "Hi, Daddy." It never gets old. Each time it stops me in my tracks. I take a deep breath and the rest of my day shifts me into my heart.

Chess as a Mirror of Life

I AM PRESENTLY LEARNING to play chess, after wanting to know how because of the *Queens's Gambit* movie which I, and thousands, loved. I kept thinking if I knew how to play chess how much more I'd have enjoyed this movie.

And then someone advertised free Chess lessons at a nearby restaurant and I thought 'Yes, how perfect is that.' When I have a better understanding and some experience under my belt, I'm going to watch the movie once again.

From what I have learned so far about chess, for me, chess equals life. There is a beginning, middle, and an end game. It hit me hard that I was in my end game. I am no longer middle-aged. For anyone who wants to argue this with me, reality says middle age would be me living to 164. I always said I was getting older, but now I think I've graduated to 'old.'

Chess has become a wake-up call to be aware of my actions. Why? Because every action you take in chess, every move you make in life, has consequences immediately and into the future.

I'm not very good at it yet. I need to practice and learn to stretch my mind and see my own moves down the road as well as 'others' moves, be it offense or defense.

I spent the better part of my life pleasing others, so I was outer-focused. I was (and am) a good girl and now need to be careful as my words, my actions, have consequences for me and others.

I find chess a mind-calming experience that supports paying attention to myself and others' moves. The best strategy can go off the track because your opponent took an unexpected tactic. Now you have to start over in your thinking. This is just like life. Sometimes we need to have a Plan B in life or even a Plan C or D at times.

My lesson here, among others, is to be more aware of my moves—actions—in life since they have consequences beyond my self-centered thoughts. For sure I'll become a better human on the planet, something as simple as saying yes when I mean yes, and no when I mean no. There are fallouts both ways. What was once so simple suddenly has meaning and future impact.

Moving any pawn into play at first is easy. The next move or the one after that is what becomes significant.

The players in the game of chess have various roles, i.e., to move in one direction only, some can move only one square at a time. Sometimes they are willing to give up one player for a strategic next move or set up for a move after that.

To me the players represent belief systems, some limiting going only in one direction one turn at a time.

For instance, my father's approach to life was like that of a pawn in chess. He could take the two steps only on the first move of each pawn, but after that, only one step at a time as stated in the rules. He was comfortable following these rules, and he applied this way of thinking to our family. Take things one step at a time.

Just as chess players might sacrifice a piece to get an advantage later, in life, people sometimes let go of certain beliefs temporarily to get ahead in the long run. This is like a chess move that might not seem important now but sets things up for success or failure later.

Pawns can be promoted into other pieces (except another pawn or king) by advancing to the other side of the board. My father would never have attempted to think ahead or had the wherewithal to move across the board. He wouldn't take the risk or even think outside the box in which he lived.

While he was as limited as the pawn, he did his best and the only way he knew how, passed down from his father. Neither of these men had the ability to consider the consequences of their actions. If only they had played chess back in the early 1900s.

Well, according to Google, human beings have been playing some version of chess for more than 1,400 years. It's one of the oldest and most widely played games in the world. My dad was too busy earning money to sit still long enough to play. Chess continues to teach me that my actions have consequences. Most good chess players, I am told, can think five moves ahead. I can't do that yet, but it is a goal.

As I sit here in retrospect, what I get is how much my father wanted to come to America. Once he was in the States, he became Americanized in his food and in his sports too. He played pool, golfed, played pinochle and gin, and dressed like he thought other American men dressed. He was dressed up every day. His reasoning was, 'You never know when company is coming. So, you need to be prepared.' My parents both had an investment in looking good at all times.

Afterthoughts

I WANT TO REMEMBER this process of writing because I feel there is more to it than what is written here; that something underneath, deeper, is a story about me that I am now ready and willing to see.

I want to remember how it felt to take care of my father. I was just doing it automatically. There was no time to think or feel. There was no one else to do it. I was taught respect and responsibility, and it was what I was to do.

I want to remember what it felt like when he threw me a bone. Do I settle for crumbs in life? Am I not worth it and thus any little bit is OK? Do I have relationships with men and women like I had with my father? Walking on eggs, frightened of his tongue or his belt?

I learned a long time ago when there was a period in my life when I was beaten and thought I deserved it. When asked if I think children should be beaten, of course I'd say no. And yet I did to my kids, not with a belt, with a slap, or with punishment, but beat them with my mouth, my words, my tone of voice.

I learned to be a rageaholic from my father. I learned how to shut down, to go into my head where it was safer than my heart. Maybe his not talking to me when I was growing up, or my lack of memory about it, is because I was too afraid to speak for saying the wrong thing. What was OK one day and I got a 'good girl' for, I got smacked for the next. That I never had a chance to be a child, only a non-fidgeting little person who had to say no to anything offered.

Do I deserve more? Do I think I am less than human and don't need to be treated well? Do I go after emotionally unavailable relationships to honor my father in some way?

"Does someone have to die for me to get the lesson?" Tony, my late ex-husband, asked me this question when my mother died. I never got the love my little inside girl wanted and yet, my mother told me how much she loved me. So maybe the answer is yes, that's what it took. What does it take now? Only time will tell.

When do I become my own person? Not who you want me to be, but who I want to be—and I don't know who that is because I've always been who you want me to be, and I want you to love me, so I do it willingly.

Did I get the love? I don't think so. I'm talking here about unconditional love, not 'if you do this, then I'll love you.' The only unconditional love I've ever experienced came from my children, Tony, and my dogs, Brownie and Melody. And there was no unconditional love from myself to me before writing this memoir.

I used to look in the mirror and see all that was wrong with me, not all that was right with me. I have to tell on myself and remember my blessings when I look in the mirror now, not my perceived shortcomings. I see what is right with me.

I've been taught to live in the question since it provides multiple answers. Once I have an answer, I stop asking the question. Sometimes it's helpful to keep asking the question, creating options for ourselves.

Writing this memoir has freed me from the past and has given me peace and healing I didn't even know I wanted, let alone needed, or even knew existed.

Quite honestly the outcome surprised and pleased me at the same time. Surprised me because I always thought of my dad as a mean, angry, out-of-control, cruel tyrant of a man. It turns out that many of these stories smack of love and softness and I am willing to receive it. I stand with upraised hands to welcome it into my life, albeit it these many years later. It's never too late to reframe the past.

I am now able to live in the present and put my past to rest. Do I do this perfectly? Of course not. I still have old memories that get triggered. Today I can look at them, thank them for whatever contribution they made to me way back when, and let them go. Forgive them as I forgive myself.

Writing this book showed me all the time we spent together—surprised me actually. At the same time, my perception of my childhood has been positively shifted. I can see my father differently. I can see my childhood differently. I can see myself differently.

Why this book?

I wrote this book originally for my father, to get the stories told, so my family and friends could know who he was.

As I write I find that there is healing taking place I didn't expect, asked for, or even thought possible. Some endings occur that are far beyond what I would have expected, yet all are good.

The stories inform me that there were so many interactions with my father who I thought I never saw much because he worked so hard, but the stories don't lie.

Why did I write it? Is it for my father who has been gone a long time now? Do I write it to simply to say I wrote it? Is it for my children who know only a few of these vignettes? Do I write it for my ego to get money and prestige for it? Is it, at its core, truly a legacy? Or did I write it for readers to get motivated, moved, or touched by these stories and take action in their own lives? To make peace with their past and themselves?

Why am I so surprised it's got happy endings when he was such a tyrant? Maybe it's true he had no training in Loving Father 101. Did he just do what he had experienced himself? Was he influenced by my mother, who didn't seem to know how to give love either?

What am I to learn here? What is beneath the surface that I have not seen or felt or experienced? That I was loved and didn't know it? Yes, that's the easy answer.

What's the truth under it all? Do I need to forgive them and show compassion? Yes, they did the best they knew how. But what about the little girl who didn't feel loved. For sure they'd say they loved me, but it was a tell, not a show. I wanted and still want the show.

Maybe these stories are the show. If there were a common thread it is love, compassion, respect, integrity, forgiveness, reconciliation, and a sense of humor. Truth be told, it's not at all what I expected.

What if it is me who wasn't able to receive the love because it didn't look or feel a certain way? It doesn't excuse them, what happened happened, but I'm not lily white here. I participated in the interactions even as a child. I knew if I went to my father he'd give me most anything

I wanted (except for a pony). I wouldn't even bother to ask my mother. I expected she'd say no.

But that's the past. If they were here today, I'd approach them much differently. First, I'd ask a lot of questions of not only my childhood, but theirs. I'd ask them if they'd do anything different given the choice. In my heart of hearts, I think they'd ask for my forgiveness for the harm they did to an innocent child. I think I'd ask their forgiveness to not trust they loved me because it didn't fit my pictures.

What if I need to forgive myself as well as them and that the memoir is about that forgiveness and having peace, freedom, and release from the past? If so, for the rest of my life I can live in the present.

Is that what the book was all about for me to get to this realization? That they did do the best they could, and while I still have brokenness inside, I am a miracle today. Yes, I did the work, but they instilled something in me that allowed me to do it, to go for it not knowing what I'd find out.

What I get is that my childhood was a 'tell' not a 'show' which doesn't mean they didn't love me. It means they showed it the only way they knew how. Not my way, their way. If it doesn't look a certain way, does it mean it's not so? No. I must be open to receiving however it comes, not try to control the delivery. Use my gut for its authenticity. My gut can be trusted.

My perceptions can shift, my defenses can be lowered, and I can see this differently. Just writing this brings me peace, love, and joy.

What can I see differently? What if he knew no other way? Maybe he wished he were different. Maybe he wished he knew what to say. Maybe he was brought up in an era where you didn't speak to your children as people. Maybe he was brought up by animals. I do know this last sentence wasn't true.

Yet I don't want to forget my brokenness, but rather, to reframe it. In Japan The Perfect Imperfection is called *kintsugi*, meaning "golden joinery."

Wikipedia reports this is their art of repairing broken pottery by mending the areas of breakage with gold dust and lacquer. It shows that 'scars' are not something to be hidden with shame, but to be displayed with pride.

My 13 Ways to Heal

THE THIRTEEN METHODS I used in no particular order in this process include:

1. Accepting each of my parents, children, husbands, friends as he or she or they were, having done the best they could with what they had at the time.

2. Forgiving me for my participation in the conflicts.

3. Forgiving my father/mother/husband.

4. Shifting my perceptions. I can see this differently.

5. Asking myself, 'How important is this?'

6. Letting it go.

7. Compassion for what he/she didn't know.

8. Finding love, softness, and peace.

9. Remaining open to possibilities.

10. Remembering the special moments.

11. Acknowledging and welcoming divine intervention.

12. Trusting the process.

13. Didn't stop before the miracle(s).

Today my mantra is I live in the land of abundance and the space of possibility. I am a work in progress. I am at choice today as to how I respond to situations and people. Writing this memoir has reinforced all I have endured and am healing from. Am I healed? I can report I am certainly on the path.

My 'good girl' has grown up and is now age appropriate. I am a recovering good girl, which makes me smile. What does this mean? It means, to me, that I have choices today and most often I make good ones.

Acknowledgements

You wouldn't be reading this book today were it not for some very dedicated and supportive people. My coach, Andrew, who was my supportive, patient cheerleader from the get-go, my developmental editor, Shavonne Clarke, Leslie Leyland Fields and the loving and supportive writing community of *Your Story Matters* and my *selfpublishing.com* family. I also include The Magnificent Four and my DR family. And last but certainly not least, my go-to person, Jacqui Bishop, who was on this roller coaster ride with me from the start. And lastly, the support of my family, Kevin, Kim, and Lauren, my granddaughter, who encouraged and supported me throughout this process.

Developmental edits and proofreading by Motif Edits—www.motifedits.com